Land Contract Homes

For Investors

❧❧

Michael Delaware

If, And or But
Publishing Company

Published by
'If, And or But' Publishing Company
P.O. Box 2559
Battle Creek, Michigan 49016 USA
www.ifandorbutpublishing.com

ISBN-13: 978-0615925684 (If, And or But Publishing)
ISBN-10: 0615925685

This book also contains clipart illustrations which were
acquired by means of royalty free usage rights in 2013
and are copyright to: *GraphicsFactory.com* on pages:
1,3,5,12,19,21,23,25,27,31,35,39,44,47,48,51,53,57,58,60,
63,64,67 & 71. All other illustrations are copyright to *If,
And or But Publishing.*

While attempts have been made to verify all information
provided in this publication; neither the author nor the
publisher assumes any responsibility for errors,
omissions, or contrary interpretations of the subject
matter herein. The views expressed are those of the
author alone, and should not be taken as expert
instruction or commands.
This book is sold with the understanding that neither the
author nor the publisher is engaged in rendering legal,
accounting, or other professional advice. If legal or other
expert assistance is required, the services of a competent
person should be sought.

In Memory of
Andre Delaware

Table of Contents

Introduction

❧

Before proceeding, it is important to make a necessary disclaimer concerning legal advice. None of the information contained in this book is intended to constitute legal or other professional advice. You should not rely solely on the information contained in this book for making legal decisions.

It is recommended one consult with an attorney or other professionals for specific advice tailored to your situation in the area of which you are doing business.

The information contained herein has been obtained through sources deemed reliable but cannot be guaranteed as to its accuracy. Any information of special interest should be obtained through independent verification. Real Estate laws vary from state to state, so always consult competent legal professionals in your area.

After releasing the first book about Land Contracts in December 2012, entitled: *Understanding Land Contract Homes: In Pursuit of the American Dream* I began to draft this book designed specifically for the investor.

The first book was directed at the subject of Land

Contracts in general, and I would recommend reading that one first, before reading this one. This book is a supplement to the first one, and will concentrate on the investor perspective on the subject. Its focus is the use of Land Contracts as an investment tool.

Land Contracts, also known as *'Contracts for Deed'* and other names in various states across the U.S. refers to essentially *seller financing.* The seller of the home holds the note for the property until all the terms have been met in the agreement, including payment and settlement, and then transfers full title to the individual buying.

Understanding how to best use a Land Contract for the purpose of maximizing your investment possibilities is what will be discussed chapter by chapter in this book. The use of a Land Contract in selling investment property is a great way to receive a return on your investment, as well as help other people achieve the goal of home ownership.

Chapter One:

Profit & Purpose

જ્જ્જ

When many investors read this material, their thoughts will immediately wander to the profitability of Land Contracts with investment property. Although profit is essential to being able to survive in such an activity, one should also never lose sight of the greater purpose behind this, which is making it possible for a buyer to become a home owner.

Certainly there are many home buyers that choose to go with a Land Contract purchase are attempting to buy *now*, while their credit is shaky, and re-finance later. However, as an investor one should never lose sight of the fact that you are providing them an opportunity that they would not have been able to take on without your help. So it is not only about running a profitable business, it is also about

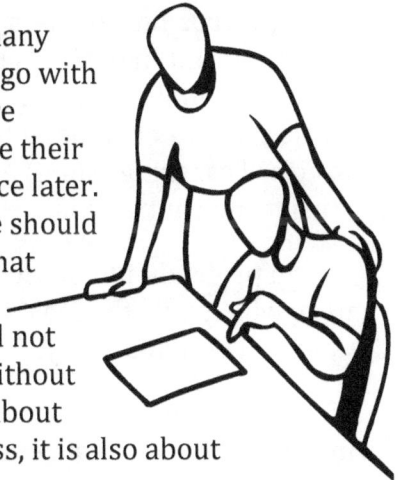

helping people.

"If your conduct is determined solely by considerations of profit you will arouse great resentment."

- Confucius

Likewise, in the current political climate in the U.S. the media has been engaging in a campaign as I write this book to champion the cause of higher taxation to 'Make the rich pay their fair share'. This campaign has evolved to target anyone who is profitable in business to be without a soul. Not wanting to engage in any debate about politics, I merely want to point out that the word 'profit' in today's society has for some become more of a slur, than a necessary fact of doing business. History has many examples of the prosperous being assaulted for their success, even though it is profit that turns the future wheels of commerce.

The truth is, no business survives without profit. To try to run a no-profit business, one would ultimately collapse whenever the first emergency occurred. Profits offer the cushion for reserves to protect a business from the unexpected. It also offers business resources in which to expand. Profit in business permits endurance, without it, there is no endurance. There is a basic law in the universe that either something expands, or it ultimately contracts. Few things survive very long as a flat line of no expansion, no contraction.

So profit should be viewed as that outcome in any venture which puts the most important thing there for the survival of that activity: *future.*

Can you imagine feeling very enthusiastic about losing over and over again every time you invested in something? Would you consider that you would continue to do that into the future? Of course not! You would experience a failure or two, and sensibly move onto some other activity with more future in it. To do otherwise is to go bankrupt. People by nature prefer to win than lose.

In professional sports, a coach or manager only survives the long term in his or her job by winning, not by losing. Sure, one can lose a game, or even have a losing streak, but *too long* a losing streak will soon find the powers that be changing coaches or managers.

So in business, the same thing happens. Lose too much money in one direction for too long, and soon the incoming money stops coming in and the venture collapses. One could therefore argue that to demonize 'profit' is to become the bridesmaid to bankruptcy in fact. Sure, many businesses struggle for years, and have narrow profits, or gradient progressive losses. Ultimately however, they either endure with profit or they eventually collapse with negative returns.

So never be afraid of profit as an investor. Profit is a good thing. It means you can continue to invest in the thing that made you the profit. In the business of selling Land Contract homes, it means that you can help more people become homeowners, and experience the American Dream. Never lose sight of that purpose. If you can do that, you will have taken the first step to success with this activity.

Where 'profit' becomes the target of controversy and negativity is when it achieved through dishonesty.

Always be upfront in anything you do with this business, make sure both parties understand what they are agreeing to, and you can not only avoid a lot of legal situations, but build a popular reputation of being an honest person to do business with. The easiest way to do this is to never lose sight of the purpose of helping others.

Chapter Two:

Investment Potential

ॐ∞

What kind of investment potential is there in selling a home to another on a Land Contract? There are many factors that enter into this equation. However, I have chosen to list out the three most important areas to consider in this for the prospective investor:

1) Equitable Re-sale value

2) Earnings from Interest

3) Realized gain from Default

Let's examine each one of these independently.

Equitable Re-Sale Value

In examining the investment potential in equitable re-sale value, we are taking into consideration the acquisitions costs incurred to you as the investor, versus what you sell it for. So for example, let's assume you purchased a home as a foreclosure that was in a neglected condition for the price of $50,000 in the example below.

Then, you spent additional dollars on top of that to repair or restore the home to a livable condition. In this example, let's project that you budgeted and spent $15,000 doing that. Your net investment in this example is a total of $65,000.

Now assuming you did proper market research to begin with, let's say that you have determined that the average marketable value in the area for a home of comparable design, bedroom count and location is between $80,000 to $85,000 on average. One can extract from a straight cash sale of the home at the price of $80,000 would net you a profit of $15,000 on your investment. So the investment potential for equitable re-sale value could be said to be approximately 18 3/4% over your initial investment.

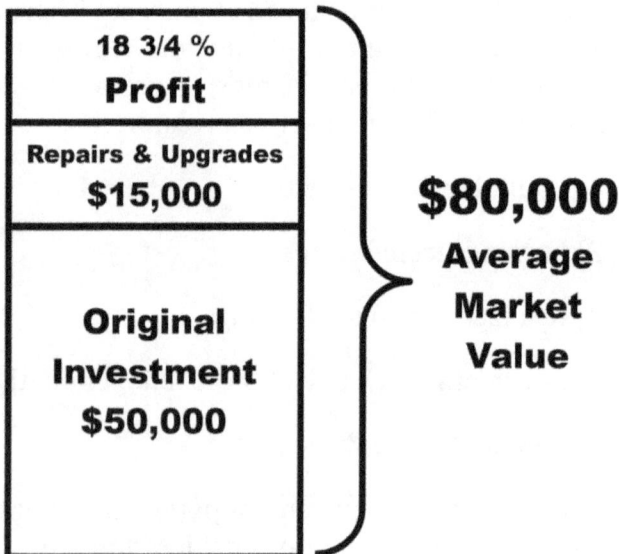

18 3/4 % **Profit**
Repairs & Upgrades **$15,000**
Original **Investment** **$50,000**

$80,000

Average Market Value

To calculate this, one takes the final re-sale value and subtracts the initial investment, which gives you the final number for the profit. In the example given here, that would be:

$80,000 - $65,000 = $15,000

Then one takes the profit of $15,000 and divides this number by the total re-sale value again.

The formula then becomes $15,000 divided by $80,000 equals percentage of gain, or more exactly:

$15,000/$80,000 = .1875 (18 3/4 %)

In a perfect world of re-selling a home in real estate one should always seek to sell it for more than your original net investment. However, in some cases, it might be necessary or better to ignore a high equitable re-sale return, and accept a narrow percentage, a break even return or a sales price below that of the initial investment in order to sell the home. Why would anyone do this?

That brings us to the next factor to examine in investment potential: *Earnings from Interest.*

Earnings from Interest

When one sells a home on Land Contract, there are two component parts to this seller financed loan: *Principle* and *Interest.* These are defined as follows:

Principle: The sum of money owed in a debt.

Interest: A charge for a loan in the form of a percentage of the amount owed.

When one structures a Land Contract, there is always the defined agreed upon purchase price, which become the principle in the seller financed note. The next factor is the interest both parties agree to for the seller extending credit to the buyer.

Each payment the buyer makes in the agreement consists of both a portion of interest and principle. The interest is said to be 'Amortized' over time. 'Amortized' means the payment off of a debt in installment payments over time. It comes from the Latin phrase *Ad Mors,* which literally means *'To Death'* or *'Put to death'.*

Essentially to amortized a loan is to define how it is put to death, or paid off. Therefore all loans have what is known as an 'Amortization schedule' which defines the breakdown of the duration of the loan, the number of payments required in total. It also represents the breakdown of principle and interest payments.

In this illustration, you will see that the portion of principle versus interest payments over time. You will also see in the gray area that the portion of the payments for the earlier payments consists of a greater percentage of interest, and the lesser percentage of principle. As the loan moves forward in time, these percentages invert and towards the end of the time frame the payments towards principle become the larger portion.

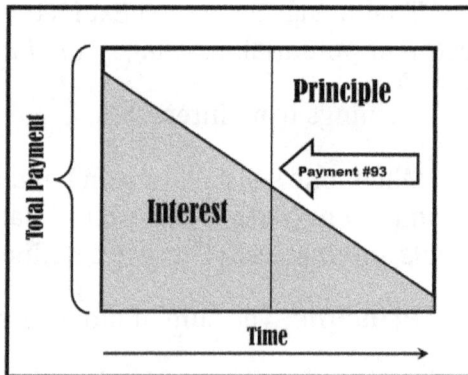

Amortization of a loan structures the payments to

always first pay the investor their interest on their money, and later the return of principle.

Interest is compounded on the remaining balance. As each payment is made, it is calculated upon the remaining balance minus the principle paid from the prior payment.

With the payments structured with a majority of the interest paid in the earliest portion of the loan, one can see from the above example that the buyer will pay a larger price over time for the home than if they had paid directly with outright cash on the initial purchase.

Another factor that impacts ones consideration on interest as investment potential is the final numbers of interest gained over the life of the loan. Let's examine the total interest a seller would receive in a land contract paid over 15 years on a financed note of $50,000 at 10% interest.

Take a look at this illustration representing an amortization schedule for such a loan:

Month	Payment	Interest	Principle	Balance
1	$537.30	$416.67	$120.63	$49,879.37
2	$537.30	$415.66	$121.64	$49,757.73
3	$537.30	$414.65	$122.65	$49,635.08
4	$537.30	$413.63	$123.67	$49,511.41
5	$537.30	$412.60	$124.70	$49,386.71
6	$537.30	$411.56	$125.74	$49,260.97
7	$537.30	$410.51	$126.79	$49,134.18
8	$537.30	$409.45	$127.85	$49,006.33
9	$537.30	$408.39	$128.91	$48,877.42
10	$537.30	$407.31	$129.99	$48,747.43
11	$537.30	$406.23	$131.07	$48,616.36
12	$537.30	$405.14	$132.16	$48,484.20

One can see that the monthly payment to the seller each month is $537.30.

Over the life of the loan, the payments include a portion of both interest and principle, as described earlier. However, when one combines the entirety of the interest payments over the life of the loan, to grand total is: $46,714.00.

To arrive at the total payments on this one takes the length of the loan (In this case 15 years) and multiplies this by 12 months.

15 years X 12 months = 180 total payments.

Then take the total number of payments (180) and multiply that by the monthly payment of $537.30.

180 X $537.30 = $96,714.00

Subtract the original re-sale value of $50,000 and one gets the total interest paid.

$96,714.00 - $50,000 = $46,714.00.

If one compares it to the agreed upon re-sale value of $50,000 as defined in the original purchase, one can see the amortized investment potential if one were to assume the investor paid $35,000 originally for the home, and another $10,000 to repair and perform upgrades.

Compare this with earnings in the illustration on the next page:

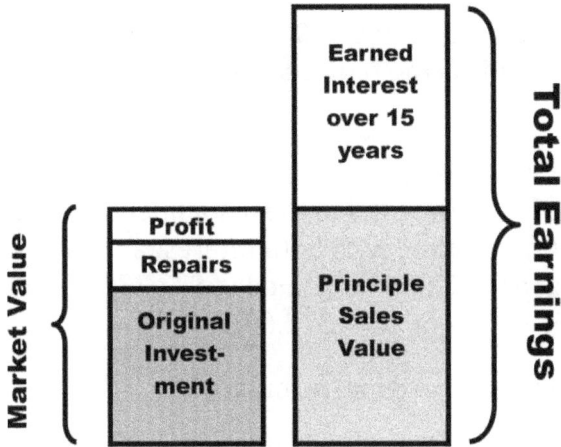

So an investor must also examine not only the re-sale value, but also the investment potential if the earned interest over the life of the loan. One can see by this illustration below that by payment #93 one has recovered their initial investment from the buyer through interest and principle payments, and the remaining principle balance is still quite large.

Therefore if the buyer re-finances the loan after 5 years (60 payments of $537.30) the remaining principle

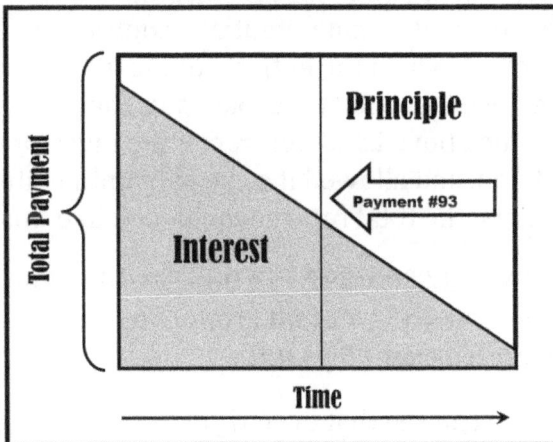

balance would be $40,460.00 per the amortization schedule. This is the required to be paid off to settle the loan.

If you add the pay-off amount at the projected 5 year mark, and the total of the installment payments to that point, complete with both interest and principle, one arrives at a final amount gained of $32,238.00 (60 X $537.30) + $40,460.00 = $72,698.00.

Using the original formula of:

Total Earnings - Original investment = *Profit*

We now see that it becomes:

Total Earnings (Principle + Interest at time of sale) - Original Investment = *Profit*

In this case it looks like this:

$72,698.00 - ($35,000 purchase + $10,000 repairs) = $27,698.00 Profit (Approximately 38% total return over 5 years)

Of course if you choose to keep the Land Contract in place or renew it, it can potentially continue on to full amortization, in which the entirely of the interest would be received over the life of the loan, plus the principle. In the case of the above Land Contract if the investor did not have a balloon, and allowed it to be paid until maturity in 180 payments, the total return would look like this:

180 X $537.30 = $97,714.00 - ($35,000 Purchase + $10,000 repairs) = $51,714.00 Profit (Approximately 53% total return over 15 years)

So one can see that even if you sell a home for the

same or less than what you have originally invested in the home, one can still realize a profit through interest over time.

Here is an illustration that exemplifies that:

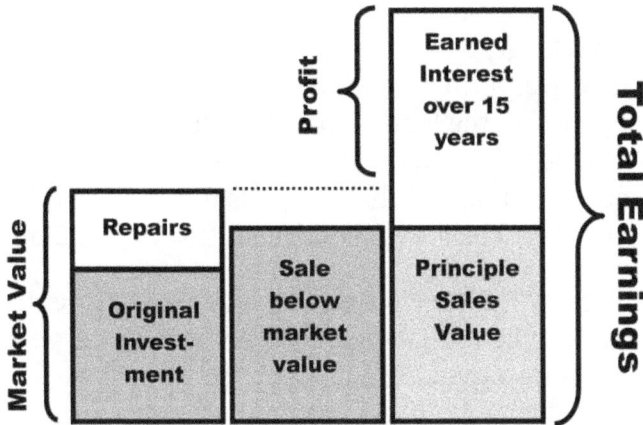

In this above example, the home was sold for less than what was originally invested, however in the long term the profits from interest far exceeded the original investment.

So what happens if the buyer skips out and does not fulfill the Land Contract agreement, and essentially goes into default? Let's examine this next.

Realized Gain from Default

A buyer going into default on a Land Contract is not uncommon. Things happen, people lose their jobs, experience the death of a bread winner, and cannot work due to some illness or disaster, and fail to perform on the Land Contract.

From the perspective of an investor, is this really a bad thing? It may sound so, and certainly there is some loss experienced with this, particularly if they do not return the property to you in the same condition that they received it in.

However, just like when someone walks away from a mortgage, be it through foreclosure or signing the deed back over as in a 'deed in lieu' arrangement, there is no obligation on the lenders part to return any of the buyers money. In fact, the buyer loses every dollar they invested in the home. What happens to the seller? They get the property back, in a good condition or a bad one.

However, the seller retains all down payments and collected installment payments received over the years. By defaulting on the Land Contract, the buyer has surrendered all of that investment on their part.

So let's examine this with two different scenarios. The first being one where the people walked away from the home amicably, and left no damage after only performing two years on the original agreement. Your realized gain might look something like this illustration:

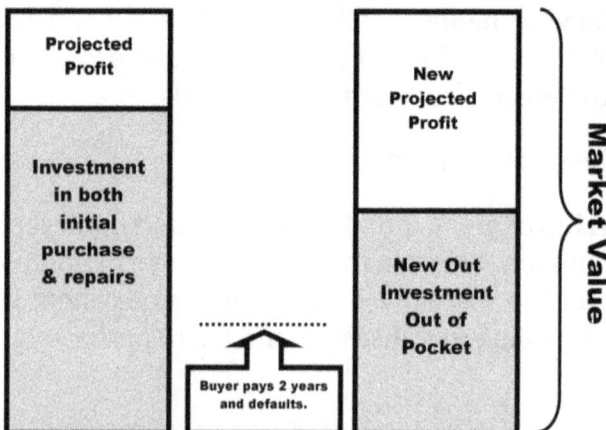

The other one might face is one where you had to pursue legal action, have them removed, and received the home back with a lot of damages. Let's look at a illustration where you might have more expenses involved after two years into the agreement:

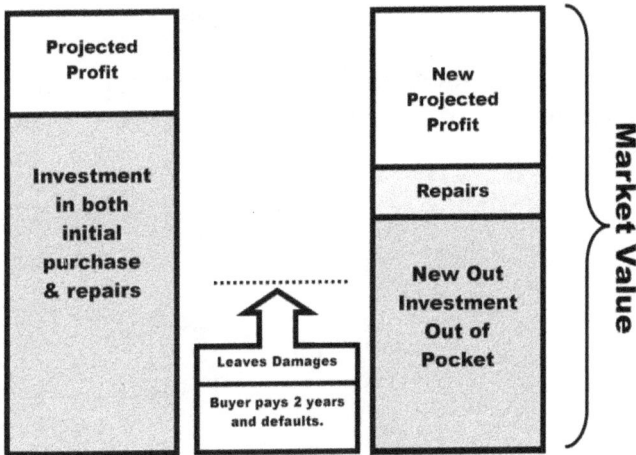

Projected Profit		New Projected Profit
Investment in both initial purchase & repairs	Leaves Damages ↑ .... Buyer pays 2 years and defaults.	Repairs
		New Out Investment Out of Pocket

Market Value

As you can see, both scenarios retained a profit for the investor, but more importantly, when the home is put back on the market again, the seller has more options. The seller having realized some gain from the former default can do any of the following again in offering a new Land contract:

A) They can place the home back on the market for the same value they sold it two years earlier.

B) They can place the home on the market for a reduced price in order to sell it more quickly, or compensate for a declining market.

C) They can place it on the market at a higher value if market values have increased in that time.

In any of the scenarios, the investor can easily realize gain from the former default, and continue forward as before with a new buyer. I have known sellers to have re-sold a home on Land Contract several times over a 5 year period, and are at present selling the home to new buyers who are performing, and they have already recovered all of their original investment.

So there is most definitely investment potential in selling residential property on a Land Contract as you can see by the examples given in this chapter.

Chapter Three:

Finding Capital

৵৵

When one is looking to begin selling homes on Land Contract, one must start somewhere with some capital to acquire the first investment home. Capital is defined as "Cash of goods used to generate income either by investing in a business or a different income property." One requires capital in some form in which to purchase real estate as an investor.

So where does one begin to acquire capital to invest? Sometimes it may require some creativity, and some borrowing, and as with any investment, there is always risk. However, if one really has confidence in the venture they are engaging in, and has done their homework in advance, the risk can be minimal. The chapters throughout this book with help you with preparation, but there is always more to learn on the subject.

Capital to invest in a home can come from a variety of sources. It basically falls into two groupings however, your money and/or someone else's money.

Spending your own money is easy. You save the cash, and use that to buy investment property. Or you borrow from your own reserves, like a loan on your own 401k or other retirement account. When you do not have the benefits of these resources, then you must seek capital from other resources.

Here is a list of possible places you could borrow money from:

Partnering up with family or friends. Your do the work, repair the home, market it and find a buyer, and they provide the capital. You get a portion of the profits, which will enable you to branch out on your own in the future if successful.

A 'Home Equity Line of Credit' (HELOC) either through a bank or credit union. This is a loan on other property you own, usually your principle residence. Banks in recent years have had tighter restrictions on HELOC loans, however you can still find them if your credit is in good shape.

Going to your bank or credit union with a business plan and applying for a business loan will sometimes be a resource, providing you have a good history with that institution and a good credit history. Smaller banks and credit unions tend to be more about relationships and are often more personal, so this can also be a good option.

If you own any other real estate free and clear of liens, and your credit is good, you can often get a new mortgage on that property and use this as investment dollars as well.

I have had some investors in recent years pull their investments from the stock market, and use those funds to buy small single family homes. Since 2006 values took a steep decline in many areas of the country, and homes in some areas have dropped in value by as much as 40 to 50% of their former values.

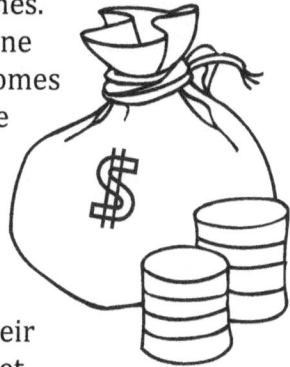

In Southwest Michigan where I have sold homes, some areas have fallen as far as 80% of their former values. With the stock market struggling as well, it is not surprising that investors are seeking real estate to acquire in their own areas. No matter the economy, people still need to live somewhere, and affordable housing is always in demand.

One can also borrow against retirement accounts, such as a 401K.

In some cases, I have seen investors use unsecured credit cards, which can be risky as the interest rates tend to be much higher than a conventional loan. However, if your credit is good, there are zero interest credit cards available which will carry no interest for as much as 12 months.

As a last resort, there are individuals that are called 'Hard Money Lenders' which offer short term loans at high interest rates. I only suggest using them in situations where you need to borrow funds in very short windows of time. The interest rates charged on these loans are often very high, and so it is not something you want to carry as a debt for a long period of time. You can find hard money lenders by researching on the Internet.

Chapter Four

Getting Started

❧❧

Where is the perfect place to start with investment property? Over the years I have wrestled with that question as it has been presented to me, and the answer that had finally come home to ring true is: *That with which you are most familiar.* That is the best place to start with investment property. *One would start with areas where you are most familiar.*

The place you grew up, or currently live. Look for homes in your neighborhood, or town. Additionally I have always considered it best to keep them within a 2 mile radius to start. You do not need to be driving long distances when renovating, as that will run costs up as well.

Following the above advice is a good guideline for shopping location, but how to you begin to locate properties in your area? The best

place to start is by contacting a local Realtor. They offer a resource called the 'Multiple Listing Source' (MLS). The MLS contains all the current properties available for sale in the area. It is a compilation of homes for sale posted by all the Realtors in that geographic area, and it includes residential, commercial and even vacant properties for sale.

When a bank is looking to sell a home because they acquired from the foreclosure of a mortgage, they make it available for sale through a local Realtor. These homes are called 'Real Estate Owned' (REO) properties, and this term REO is the common description banks describe them as across the U.S. It comes from the term used on their accounting ledgers of assets they have, and typically banks do not like to hold REO homes very long, and so sell them at a discounted price for rapid re-sale.

The U.S. Department of Housing and Urban Development (HUD) also sells homes. These are foreclosures on Federal Housing Authority (FHA) loans. They essentially are no different from other foreclosures on the market, with the exception that in order to buy them you must go through a Realtor. Also, the buying process is blind bidding though an online website. You can search for HUD homes at: **www.hudhomestore.com**

The best way to gain access to these homes as they hit the market is to be working with a local Realtor. There are so many electronic methods these days that Realtor's have available to them, that you can establish a relationship with them to receive instant emails, have access to web portholes, and other online features to look at available properties in your area. This is the best way to stay ahead of the competition, and there is a lot of competition for foreclosed homes.

It is important to know that purchasing an REO property typically requires a written offer, money down and proof of funds or financing before any offer is considered by a bank. They expect it to come through a Realtor, so it is always a good idea to have one that you like working with. I usually do not recommend using the Realtor who is listing the property for the bank to submit your offer to them, as they are not working for you, but the bank. It is likely you will get a better negotiated price if you have your own representation in transaction. However, you can use the listing Realtor if you have no other option.

Other resources for discounted investment properties are through online auction websites, or tax auctions. I highly recommend you do your homework on these properties before buying, and especially go by to do a physical inspection before bidding. Realtor's can be a great resource to find out prior re-sale values on the property in question, as well as tax rates, neighborhood sales figures, etc. A title company can also tell you if there are issues with the title.

Another resource is to seek out are estate sales. These are sales where a person has passed away and the family is trying to sell off their assets, including the real estate. Sometimes these are advertised through a Realtor, and sometimes the families advertise them for sale by owner in the local newspaper. Other times they make them available for

sale through an attorney. Another contact person to perhaps have for referrals for these is an estate attorney in your area. Setting yourself up as a willing investor directly with them might offer you the occasional deal on an estate home that you would otherwise not get a chance to acquire.

In any case, you will want to have funds available to you to purchase the homes you come across as deals, and also have funds set aside to do any necessary repairs or upgrades. Remember to also factor in related costs for a closing, such as title company fees, title insurance, inspections, and other fees that may be associated with getting clear title.

As a final note I always recommend that you purchase title insurance with any home you buy and factor that into the cost of your closing fees. Title insurance protects you in the future from someone else coming along claiming title to your property, and makes for an easier re-sale process down the road should something be discovered wrong in the title work.

Chapter Five:

Ideal Investment Homes

ॐ☙

What would be the ideal investment property for re-sale on a Land Contract? Unfortunately there is no clear cut direct answer to this question, but what you are looking for is simply a location that will be in demand. This may take some investigating in your area.

Perhaps it is a home close to a local college, or in a particular school district. Perhaps properties in your area are in higher demand near the beach, or public park, or a particular shopping district or nightlife? Never assume you know the answer if you are new to an area. Always investigate and interview people in the community.

You might even do a survey. A few hours in front of a local grocery store or two with some survey questions about the community might tell you everything you need to know.

Consulting local professionals in the area is also advisable. Realtor's can give you insight into this. Appraisers could give you insight into what would be the areas that seem to hold their values. Also talking to the local police department would give you answers to crime levels in certain areas of town. I suggest gathering as much information as you can from more than one resource to make your determination on location.

What about the physical characteristics and features of the house? From my experience in Real Estate in my market I can tell you that three bedroom homes seem to be easier to sell than two bedroom homes, and a four or five bedroom home can also be a hot seller.

Having a two car garage is generally preferable to a one car, and an attached garage is generally preferable than to a detached one. Rural homes with acreage seen to be something asked about a lot, but with rising gas prices, these can also be a liability if they are too far away from areas people might drive to work. Any property with a pole barn tends to sell quickly as well.

You might also want to consider your target audience. Are you going to be targeting an older or retired clientele? Or are you looking for single family starter homes?

I have learned over the years that as people get older they tend to want to avoid larger homes, or homes with a lot of stairs, so this would rule out two story homes for that crowd.

However, a younger family starting out with little

children might fall in love with a two story home with a basement that can serve as a playroom for the kids, etc.

So you have to examine your target audience, which may be effected by the demographics of the location you are in.

Here are some examples:

If you are going to be selling homes in a retirement community, you might want to focus on ranch homes.

If you are going to be selling homes in a vacation community, you might want to make sure it is accessible to the beach or other waterfront, or has a good view.

If you are buying in an area near an elementary school and high school you might have better success looking at homes with three bedrooms, a good sized back yard and not on a main highway.

Choosing the ideal investment property also has to do with purchase price, cost of repairs and re-sale value. You will want to make sure you are buying at a reduced price, something that is below market values for the area. You will want to be sure your repairs are budgeted and come in below budget if possible.

Finally, you will want to make sure that you can profit from the re-sale of the home to a new buyer when offering a Land Contract sale. These are all things to keep in mind when seeking the ideal investment property.

Properties with a well and/or septic system can also present concerns. Wells can requiring cleaning, and can sometimes be expensive to repair, or replace. Make sure you have it inspected before finalizing the sale; to be sure it conforms to the County code requirements. The same goes for septic systems.

A problem with a septic system can also be quite expensive to remedy. In some locations, government well and septic violations can affect the transfer of title to a property, so always inspect, or require the seller to provide a passing well and septic inspection before finalizing the sale.

Chapter Six:

Marketing

❧

When you have purchased a home, and have done your remodeling, where is the best place to market it to, in order to find your Land Contract buyers? I should perhaps re-word that question to 'Where do you find the Land Contract buyers you want'?

When you place an advertisement in the newspaper, and simply make available a Land Contract home, you will get calls. You may even get so overwhelmed with calls that you get frustrated, as all the prospects will seem very interested, but you will find out many are unqualified.

The trick with marketing is such a home it to target your ideal applicant by setting the proper advertisement out there. If you

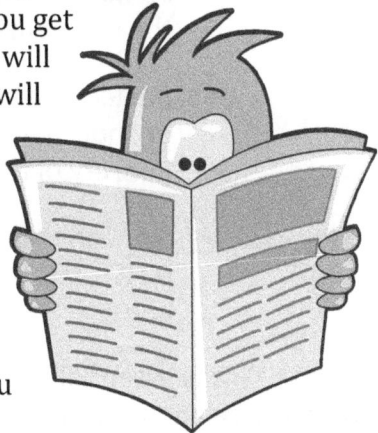

make a simple advertisement that reads like the following:

Land Contract Home for Sale
123 Forest Street
$50,000
Call George 555-555-5555

This will surely blow your phone up with calls if it is in a desirable area, but you will spend a lot of your time going through applicants who are not going to be someone who will be your best prospect, as the advertisement it too general.

So in order to write the perfect advertisement that will ring the phone with qualified prospects, one must first define what an ideal prospect is. So what is an ideal prospect to market to for a Land Contract home?

Here is a short list:

- Someone who has a down payment, preferably 10-20% of the purchase price.

- Someone who has income that can make the payments.

- Someone whose income is not temporary or short lived, but will be stable through the entirety of the contract.

- Someone who will not destroy the home, or turn it into something unlivable like a meth house.

This is essentially what you are looking for. You do not care about much else. The first two can be screened simply by stating the terms in the advertisement. The last two can be screened by the simple statement in the ad that reads something like: "$25 application fee for finance and background check required."

So your new advertisement might read something like this:

Land Contract Home for Sale
123 Forest Street
$50,000
$5000 down payment & $400 a month payments, with a 5 year balloon.
$25 application fee for finance/background check.
Call George
555-555-5555

Will you still get some unqualified applicants? Certainly you will. However, your percentage of qualified applicants will improve dramatically over the first ad listed above, and the time you will spend will be greatly reduced in finding the right person.

People reading the ad will see the terms. They will also see that they have to apply, and have a background check.

If you do not want to sell the home yourself, you can also hire a Realtor. They will charge a commission for doing so, but they will also deal with all the calls and the advertising too. They can advertise and hold open houses through the MLS, and other publications, and reach prospective buyers. A Realtor can also help you with the purchase contracts and all the legal requirements to make sure your transaction goes smoothly.

Another method of marketing your home, particularly if you get a lot of them, would be to create your own website and take applications electronically online.

Where are good publishing resources to advertise your Land Contract Home?

Here is a short list of suggestions that I have found to be successful:

Paper classified ads in small newspapers (hometown or community papers, not the big ones with wide distribution).

Craigslist - Just be careful with the type of response you get from this one, and read the sections Craigslist makes available on the subject of being alert to scams.

Online classifieds in larger newspapers that cover the area.

Fliers with a photo of the house, terms, etc. (Post at public places, like grocery stores, etc.)

Simply placing a sign with basic terms in the front yard of the home itself.

Chapter Seven:

Screening Applicants

ಎಲ

So now you have some applicants who have called, what do you do next? You will need them to fill out an application. There are tons of basic generic applications you can buy online or through an office supply store. You are looking for information on their employment, income, etc.

Also to obtain credit history you will need their name and social security number. There are companies online that do credit checks for land lords, and they usually charge a flat fee for an application. You can also contract with those companies to have the applicant apply online, and you receive the report.

The most important information to be informed of when selling a home is to make sure you are cognizant of Fair Housing laws. One cannot discriminate based on someone's race, religion, sex, national origin, age, marital status or sexual orientation, nor can you ask about any of that on an application or suggest it in an advertisement. Fair Housing laws are always being updated, and some are more stringent at State level as well, so make sure you research this online and become familiar with them.

I always recommend that the application for the home include the terms you are offering, and making it known that you require a down payment in writing. You should ask for references, and recommend that at least one of those references be former landlords, if possible. I always call references.

One would think that the applicant will always put down *favorable* references, and so it is a waste of time. I cannot tell you how many times I have called the references given and gotten an earful from that reference on how that person damaged their home, skipped out on rent, owes them money, etc. It is truly amazing the amount of self-destructing references some applicants will provide.

Another important thing to require is a background check. This is simply a public records check on the person. Public records are available to anyone. It is important to get the current address and former addresses of the person within the last 2 years to do this.

You can go to the court house yourself, and search public records, or hire someone else to do it. What will public records reveal that will be useful for you as a seller? It may reveal a criminal history of drug manufacturing, arson, or other heavy crimes which might be a threat to your property for certain.

However, it may also reveal things like

garnishments on wages or child support, which can adversely affect how you review their monthly income. I have had applicants with good solid income which I never checked the public records whom I have had to evict as a landlord for non-payment of rent. Why? They had good solid income, but 90% of it was garnished from child support and other debts, but this was carefully omitted from their application. I used to have blind faith in the goodness of people, but years of business experience has taught me that it is okay to have this faith, but to never forget to do my own due diligence on every single applicant.

Another important thing to remember is that whatever process you set for reviewing applicants, you must follow the exact same steps on each and every applicant. If you do not, you could be charged with discrimination at some point for being strict on some, and not strict on others. So set a review process in place; create a checklist if necessary, and follow each step with everyone and you will be okay.

Chapter Eight:

Written Agreements

ஒ௸௸

Whenever you are selling a home, a preliminary step to having all parties sign on the Land Contract is to have the agreement with terms of sale in writing. If you use a Realtor, they will help you with the legal purchase agreements and required disclosures in your area.

If you choose to do this yourself, I would suggest you start with a basic purchase agreement. A purchase agreement would outline who the parties are, what the agreed upon sales price is, what the terms of the sale are (The amount being put down, payments, etc.) and details on what each party is going to be responsible for. Responsibilities that need to be defined include closing fees, insurance, escrow, taxes, title verification and inspections.

Other things that may be included in the contract could be home warranties, repairs, and personal property that may be on the premises. The agreement should also address timelines for when all these actions are to be done, and by whom. The day of final closing should also be defined in the agreement to make sure there is a target all parties are working towards. This day of closing is when the money changes hands, and the final Land Contract agreement is signed.

Federal law requires that all parties in the sale of residential real estate sign a lead based paint disclosure if the home was built before 1978. The buyer is given a disclosure on this by the seller, and is given an opportunity to pay for additional lead based paint inspections if they desire.

Individual State laws also mandate a general 'seller's disclosure' be made available by the seller and reviewed and signed by the buyer as part of the sale. There can be other additional disclosures in each State as well, or ones that pertain to a region, and they can cover many subjects from mine shafts to U.S. Air Force flight paths to native American burial sites. Check with your local Board of Realtors or State agency that oversees Real Estate transactions for the area to find out if any are required.

Title agencies also provide a valuable service in researching a title history, and providing title insurance to each party in the transaction. I always suggest with the purchase of any real estate that one obtain title insurance, as it will offer protection for you from ever having someone come along later and claim ownership to your property, or attempting to collect liens on the former owner, etc.

Always get the agreement in writing and signed by

all parties before you move forward with the formal Land Contract. Also, as a seller, you should also request verification that the person buying has the funds for down payment; this can be a simple as presenting a bank statement showing available funds. It is also customary to require an earnest deposit from the buyer to show they are serious, and in many states any agreement is not a legal binding contract if they do not provide one.

Chapter Nine:

Land Contract Components

❧❧

The Land Contract document itself can be found through a variety of legal form suppliers on the internet. You can also find them available through local title companies and real estate offices. It is the components of the contract itself which are most important.

Some of the key components are:

- Defining the exact parties in the contract (Buyer and Seller) and who they are. There can be multiple parties or corporate entities as well.

- A complete and accurate legal description of the property being sold.

- Defining the sales price and terms, including interest payments, balloon payments, and time frames of the contract.

- How annual taxes are paid and who is

responsible for this, and how it is to be reported to the other party as proof they are paid.

- How the property is be maintained, and what defines a violation of this agreement.

- What constitutes default and what are the results if this occurs.

- When full title is to be conveyed to the buyer, and under what conditions.

There are of course many other details that can be worked into the framework of the Land Contract, such as annual well and septic maintenance if applicable, or compliance with city codes, etc. All of these details should have been defined in the original purchase agreement, and incorporated into the Land Contract so it is clear to both parties.

You can also have an attorney review the Land Contract to make sure all points are covered, and also have a Realtor and/or a title agency look at it as well.

You will also want to accompany the Land Contract with an amortization schedule, which defines the principle and interest payments throughout the life of the note.

The Land Contract should also define whether a balloon payment exists, and when that is. A 'balloon' payment is a point into the future when the entire balance is to be paid in full.

Most balloons are defined as either 2, 3, 4 or 5 years on most residential Land Contracts.

A contract that omits defining a balloon payment will be considered to be paid off when the entirely of the Land Contract has run its course.

The length of the Land Contract, therefore, will also need to be defined in the terms. Land Contracts can run anywhere from 5 to 30 years, depending on what is negotiated by the parties involved.

Chapter Ten:

Protecting Your Asset

ക്ക

For some it may be hard to consider the home you are selling your asset, but it is until the buyer fully performs on the Land Contract agreement.

As a seller on a Land Contract, until you are paid in full, you hold the deed. Other people are living in the home, making payments and can be making changes to the property, and perhaps even damaging it. So how do you protect your asset?

The first way is to make sure you protect your asset is to require a sizable down payment going into the agreement, and do not waiver on that standard. Keep funds in reserve, should you ever have to take the property back in default, and make repairs.

Over the years I have seen the aftermath of damage done by disgruntled former owners. It is amazing what they will do to a property before their departure in a form of retaliation.

I have witnessed all the cabinet doors in a kitchen snapped off their hinges, kitchen drawers smashed through windows, and even concrete poured down the toilets. There are numerous ways a person can destroy a home when they are in retaliation mode, and as sad as it is, you need to be prepared in case this does happen. Having reserve capital helps to cushion the blow, and the best way to have this reserve is to have the buyer give it to you as a form of down payment.

Also, making sure there is homeowners insurance on the house to cover the loss should a disaster ever strike, such as fire, tornado, hurricane, earthquake or any other natural or unnatural event.

Require proof of payment of this every year, or collect the funds from the buyer and make the payment yourself through managing their escrow for them. You, as the lien holder, should also be the payee in the homeowner's insurance policy in the event of total loss.

A similar threat can come about with unpaid property taxes. Unpaid property taxes can result in the house going up for a tax sale, and you could potentially lose all ownership rights. Also some municipalities will place liens on a property if the City has to intervene to mow the lawn, or resolve some appearance issue that draws neighborhood complaints.

So setting up standard arrangements where the taxes are

paid and you can verify they were is essential to peace of mind. Also making arrangements to periodically drive by and inspect, or have a neighbor call you if something unusual happens or they observe that something is neglected.

The best protection for you as the seller ultimately is to do a thorough screening of the applicant in the beginning, and as mentioned before, require the buyer to pay a 10-20% down payment.

You can choose a smaller percentage, however; the down payment should be large enough to serve as a deterrent for them going into default. Some investors refer to this as making sure the buyer has "some skin in the game". If they go into default at some future date, they lose their investment. The greater their investment, the less likely they are to default.

Chapter Eleven:

What about Default?

ಎಂಚ

What happens with a Land Contract agreement when someone stops making their monthly payments? This is referred to as 'Default'. To 'Default' on a contract is to fail to perform as agreed. The Land Contract should have defined within it penalties and actions that can be taken by the seller should the buyer default.

The best preventative measure against default is to do thorough screening before entering into an agreement, but still this cannot account for every situation that can occur in someone's life to make them miss payments.

Incidents of job loss are common. An incapacitated bread winner or even the death of the bread winner can cause this to happen as well.

These are the unpredictable facts of life, and they do happen.

My suggestion has always been to try to resolve the problem through communication with the buyer before proceeding with a legal recourse. However, one should know the legal system and set this in motion as required to prevent added time on a legal process should one ultimately have to go that route.

My procedure has always been as follows:

If the payment does not arrive on the day it is required, an instant late payment letter is mailed that same day complete with reminders of penalties, etc. You can even include a highlighted copy of the applicable areas of the Land Contract agreement on default in this letter, to remind them of what could follow.

If by the second day payment if not received, and no return communication as to why it is late, I make a phone call. If I do not make contact, I proceed without delay to #3.

If no contact by day three, I send the first required legal notice to initiate forfeiture or foreclosure proceedings (depending on what is required in your State) and send the notice *return receipt requested* through the Post Office.

Somewhere between day 2 and 5, depending on what my instinct tells me based on my prior relationship with them, I make a drive over to the house to inspect. If I find it abandoned, I verify that it is abandoned by looking in the windows, and going inside depending on the circumstances. I will then change the locks as soon as possible. If it is occupied, I try to speak with the buyers and find out what is going on and try to resolve it with communication.

I never stop the legal proceedings until the payments are made, however, I may delay taking the final steps needed to bring it before a judge if the buyer is working with me to resolve the problem.

It is always a good idea to be willing to be flexible, and re-work a contract if it is possible to do so. It can save you having to evict, do repairs and re-market the property again before you again receive a positive cash flow from it.

So I recommend always trying to keep the current agreement alive if it is possible before resorting to legal action to bring about removal and repossession of the home.

However, once I take the matter to court, and spend the money to do so, I do not stop until I am paid in full for the arrears, or regain possession of the home.

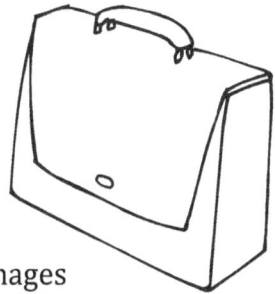

Sometimes this means that I pursue a judgment for losses and damages long after the former buyers have abandoned the home. Judgments from the court are collectible, if by no other means than garnishing their payroll and State tax returns. You would be surprised at how easy this process is, once you have gone through the steps.

Depending on which State you live in, they will either have the procedure for foreclosure or forfeiture or both to follow to regain the property. I suggest you study the laws of your State online to gain an understanding of how they work if you are going to attempt to do it yourself.

From this you will be able to make a determination on which course of action is going to be best for you. Otherwise, hire an attorney and let them handle the process for you.

Chapter Twelve:

Staying Organized

Whenever you are working with administering a Land Contract or even a rental home in residential real estate, one must maintain a sense of order in record keeping for the operation to run smoothly. Some of the essential elements have already been discussed about getting the Land Contract itself in writing, and making sure it is properly signed and notarized.

However, there are a few common areas that can be a break down for the seller if they are not organized when administering a Land contract agreement. These basic areas are:

1) Keeping a set of buyer records.

2) The escrow account.

3) Timely response on legal.

4) Marketing record keeping.

All four of these areas require that you have your files in order, and know where these records are, as well as what actions to take if you need to make use of them.

Keeping a Set of Buyer Records

What is the most important information you need to have on your buyer? Certainly a copy of the signed Land Contract agreement, and any other related documents to the sale is the obvious. However, it is very easy to omit the step of the initial application in the process as being important. This is perhaps the most important information you need on file, along with the following:

- Keep in file a copy of their ID (either a driver's license or other form of photo ID like a passport, student identification, etc.)

- A copy of their social security card.

- Copies of phone numbers for them, as well as relatives should you not be able to reach them on some future date.

- Signed agreements as to the condition of the property when they took possession. I usually recommend using a prepared checklist and have both of you fill out the information as you walk through the entire property room to room. Both of you should sign it, and have an original copy of file.

- A photographic record of the condition of the property with date stamps on the digital photos should also be on file for every room, living space, and all four sides of the home, and any other buildings on the property. This should be as thorough as you can be.

- Information on who their employer is, and ideally the address and phone numbers for this.

- The names of all the people living in the household.

Some of the above information listed is quite obvious, but some of the rest you might wonder...why? So let me go through this, and it will make sense.

The photo identification is for legal reasons, should you ever need to pursue forfeiture or foreclosure proceedings on them. Also, it is useful to have their exact legal name on file for the filing of any documents in the court, which requires correct names in legal documents.

The copy of their social security card is a common practice for verifying the person is real, and prevents the possibility of someone presenting a false identity. However, if you ever need to sue the individual at a later date, in order to collect a judgment or pursue garnishment, you will need their correct social security number.

There is no better way to make sure the one you have is correct than by having a copy of the card on file. Also, in order to pursue garnishment of wages, the employer information is a must, which explains why that is on the list.

The information about relatives is to aid you with trying to contact them when they go out of communication. Sometimes an appeal to a relative can help you bring them back into communication, and resolve any issues amicably. It is also valuable emergency information should you need to reach them, and they are not available immediately.

The signed agreement on condition is something that will enable you to prove damages to the court should you ever need to sue. The photo documentation of condition with recorded dates is also vital for presenting evidence on condition.

The names on all the people living in the household are important in some jurisdictions when pursuing evictions or forfeiture. Court documents sometimes require listing all the known occupants.

The Escrow Account

Whenever you are overseeing an escrow account, there are precise laws in each State as to how these are to be administered. Check online for the rules and regulations regarding escrow accounts in your State.

Essentially the best practice is to keep a written or digital record of each monthly deposit into the account, and semi-annual or annual disbursement from the account. These should also include hard copy records of the checks, and bills paid should you ever have the account audited.

The following are common items to be paid from an escrow:

- Village or City Property taxes.

- County property taxes.

- State property taxes.

- Homeowners Insurance.

- Flood Insurance.

- Specialty Insurance for a given area (Such as 'Wind' or 'Hurricane' Insurance.)

- Homeowners Association fees (if required).

Timely Response on Legal

In order to be effective with a timely response to a late payment or outright default on the Land Contract, it is important to know the exact legal forms required to be filed with the courts for your area. It is also important to know in advance whether you will choose to pursue forfeiture or foreclosure.

I recommend having copies of all the legal late notices, and other related court forms on hand and in an accessible location in your files.

Additionally, having some prepared letters for the event of delinquency, and print them out, sign them and make a copy of each time you use them and keep them on file under the name of that buyer/client.

I also suggest that you mail every letter with either a 'proof of mailing receipt' or even a 'return receipt requested' from the Post Office, as opposed to sending items certified or registered mail. Certified or Registered mail requires that the recipient sign for the letter, and in my experience, when they are knowingly in default, they will not sign for anything. In most cases, the court will accept a proof of mailing receipt, but I suggest you check with the County Clerk in your area to be certain.

Keeping a recorded trail of mailed receipts and letters is essential to have on file should the matter move forward to full forfeiture proceedings or foreclosure. If you skip one of these steps and do not have proper proof to present to the courts that the buyer was notified of the delinquency, you can lose precious time in having to go back and repeat steps already done.

It is also recommended that you write down and file written records of dates and times you called the buyer, and what was discussed in each call as a sort of log book. This kind of record keeping shows the courts that you have made an effort to resolve the matter with the buyer. I suggest some kind of date stamp on each written entry as well.

Timing is everything when it comes to turning the wheels of legal action. Losing time through omitted or forgotten steps can cost you weeks or months of delay in the process of regaining your asset and being able to get it back on the market for re-sale. Always be diligent, and keep accurate records, and know the rules in your State thoroughly and it will make your life so much easier.

If record keeping is not your thing, then perhaps

you can also consider hiring a professional firm to administer the Land Contract collections each month for you, or hire an accountant to help you.

You can also hire an Attorney to take on any legal proceedings necessary, but this can be costly so I always recommend doing as much that you can on your own, and only go this route for specific actions when it is beyond your area of expertise.

Marketing Record Keeping

When one advertises a home for sale in the newspaper, it is always a good idea to check the printed paper and verify your ad was published correctly. However, it is also a good practice to keep a copy of this ad on file in your records. Also keep with it a record of how many and what kind of calls you got from the ad, and how many times your ran it and where, When it comes time to run an ad again, this information will be helpful you have on file for future marketing.

I also keep with my marketing records contact information on applicants that reached out to me after I already had the home sold or rented. This makes future marketing so much easier when you can make a few phone calls first to see if there is still interest, before you spend money on new advertising.

Chapter Thirteen

Selling Early

છ~એ

What if you have a Land Contract sale on a home, and time passes and you decide you would like to liquidate and regain your capital? One option is to sell the Land Contract to another investor.

Typically this is done after the Land Contract has performed for a few years, and you have records to show it is a stable return to a new investor. One would then usually sell the Land Contract for a reduced rate from what the full return would be upon maturity, which can be as much as 10 to 20% less.

The reason for this is you want to be able to offer the investor who is going to use their capital to buy your existing contract with investment dollars a prospective yield of 10% to 20% on their return. At the same time, you want to be able to regain your initial investment, along with some profit.

So a Land Contract with a 5 year balloon, which has performed on payments approximately 2 years consistently, is going to have given you some return on investment (ROI), as well as offer future ROI to a new investor taking over.

Land Contracts have to be well written and documented for you to be able to sell them. This is why it is essential to make sure the exact legal description of the property is verified through a title company, and all parties have legally entered into the agreement without any issues that would make it unclear or unenforceable.

Incorrect legal descriptions, forged signatures, and false identities are just a few of the issues that could arise that would make an agreement unenforceable. This is another reason it is important to use a professional title company and pay for title insurance when closing on such a property, as well as a good reason to do background checks and thorough applications.

Most Land contract agreements provide a clause in the language of the agreement that permits the seller to sell their interests to another party. The only exception to this may be if there is original underlying debt on this, such as a mortgage.

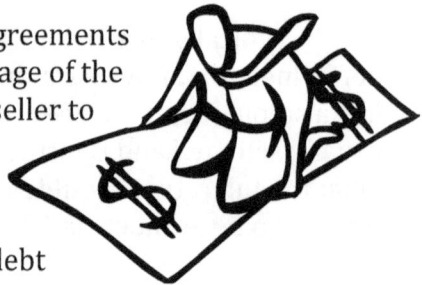

Then any sale of the Land Contract would of course have to include a settlement on the original debt before this can be an option. Depending on how much is owed on the original debt will determine as to whether this is a viable Land Contract for resale.

If one does research on the internet, you may be

able to find groups or organizations that invest in existing Land Contracts. However, the best resource for this type of buyer is going to be through active investment property groups.

One should seek out groups that hold meetings for investors, either in the community you live, the County or State and become a member. Through this kind of group you will be able to make contacts and connections that will enable you to be able to sell seasoned Land Contracts.

Why would you want to sell a Land Contract? Here are some reasons:

A) You would receive a pay-off in the form of a substantial amount immediately to accomplish other goals.

B) You no longer have to be concerned with servicing the Land Contract, as that problem now becomes the responsibility of the new investor.

C) You do not have to worry about whether the taxes or insurance are paid to protect your investment, as this is now the concern of the new investor.

D) You may make enough from the first sale if you are lucky to re-invest into one or two more homes, and repeat the process.

You can also sell part of a Land Contract by bringing on another investor to pay you off a percentage of your initial investment. You then can split the profits each month, as well as have someone else to work with to help service the Land Contract. This can also free up capital for you if you need it, and enable you to move on to other projects.

Chapter Fourteen:

Capital Gains

❦

What About Capital Gains?

Capital Gains taxes are for many investors the bane of their existence. Having to face pay that money to the U.S. Government after you assumed all the risk to make the money to begin with can be frustrating. Some may even view this as punishment, especially when one becomes disabused with how the government spends your tax dollars.

Regardless, Capital Gains Taxes are a fact of life when it comes to investing. Capital gains from a short term investment of one year or less is taxed at a rate currently in 2012 of anywhere from 10% to 35%. They are governed by the ordinary tax rate of that given year. Long term Capital Gains from assets held longer than a year is taxed at the tax bracket you are in. There are even taxes on recaptured real property, such as when you regain a home you sold on Land Contract in prior years, and the recapture rate is 25% and depends on depreciation.

A lot of confusing numbers aren't they? This is why it is best to be working with a Certified Public Accountant (CPA) when you begin investing in real estate. They are trained to stay on top of the ever-changing tax laws, and can generally keep you abreast of any tax liabilities you might face.

It may sound like a great idea to sell a remodeled home outright for cash, and take your Capital Gains hit now, and move on. However, it may also be more beneficial for you to sell the home on a Land Contract, and spread the Capital Gains tax liability out over several years.

1031 Tax Deferred Exchanges

There is also another tool that investors should become familiar with when it comes to Capital Gains taxes. There is an Internal Revenue Service code Section #1031 which permits a method of switching property and allows you to defer the Capital Gains tax until the new property is sold in the future. This is referred to as a '1031 Tax Deferred Exchange'.

The type of exchange of properties must be what is referred to as 'Like-kind' property in the IRS guidelines defined in the 1031 code. So in essence, one can sell a rental home and exchange it for another rental home or similar 'like-kind' property of equal or greater value and defer the tax from Capital Gains into the future. One can also sell several rental homes at the same time, and buy an apartment building, and defer Capital Gains taxation, provided the requirements to facilitate such an exchange are followed precisely.

Whenever one is dealing with the IRS, one must follow the rules for this procedure exactly. A particularly important rule is that a property you intend to exchange from one you are selling must be identified within 45 days, and closed within 180 days. These timelines must be adhered to, or the exchange will be considered invalid, and you will owe Capital Gains.

There are established companies around the U.S. that provide a service of managing and assisting with 1031 Tax Deferred Exchanges for a fee. It is recommended you consult with such a firm, as the IRS requires the guidelines be performed exactly for this to be permissible.

The fees you would pay for the service of facilitating a Tax Deferred Exchange is significantly less than having to pay the Capital Gains Tax on every transaction. It is permissible under the rules to essentially sell a home, and go buy one or two other homes with the proceeds from the sale, and defer the Capital Gains liability into the future, provided the IRS procedure and steps are followed.

Some investors I have come across make an art form of this, and have adopted the philosophy of the following operating plan: Defer, defer, defer, defer, defer...die. In essence, they use the 1031 Tax Deferred exchange on the sale of all of their investment properties, and continue to defer until they die, never in fact actually paying the Capital Gains Tax while they are living.

How can this impact your estate? You simply will

the properties to an heir or trust, and give the same rule book to the beneficiaries of: Defer, defer, defer, defer...die.

There are experts in the field of 1031 Tax Deferred Exchanges, and also many books written on the subject. Just from this quick review of the possibilities, any investor should become familiar with this if they ever want to expand their activities and minimize their Capital Gains liability.

Recent laws have changed regarding Roth IRA's and Self-Directed IRA's, allowing one to invest in real estate within an IRA, as well as do a complete 1031 Tax Deferred Exchange. I have included some links at the end of this book that might help you learn more about this process. I suggest that if you are interested in this that you do your own investigation into this, as opposed to relying strictly on the links provided, which are for informational purposes only.

You can also take a look at the section at the end of this book concerning useful links.

Chapter Fifteen:

Final Summary

❧∞❧

With any investment, there is risk. When looking at the subject of Land Contracts as an investment, who is to say what the future holds? Today the information in this book is the truth, and the material at present is knowledge any real estate investor can use. Tomorrow, this information may be obsolete as laws change, and so do the times.

History has shown us that man can make the rules, and also change them as he likes. Today seller financing is a permitted form of transaction in most States, however, laws can change.

During the later 1970's and early 1980's, interest rates in the U.S. climbed to as much as 18% for conventional lending. This made a Land Contract form of seller financing very popular, as

they typically offered 10% to 11% on average. In some areas of the country, this became the dominant form of financing a home. However, as interest rates eventually fell below 10% and ultimately where they languish today in a range of 3% to 4% at the time of this writing in the last few years, Land Contract use fell off for mainstream home buying.

In my first book on this subject 'Understanding Land Contract Homes in Pursuit of the American Dream' I covered the use of Land Contracts today as a means of bridging a buyer from an existing shaky credit situation to being able to repair their credit, and obtain lower interest rates offered by conventional financing. So Land Contracts have evolved with the changes in the times, and provide a great opportunity for investors.

In the world of residential real estate in 2006, there were a lot of different government programs available to home buyers that made Land contracts something of a low priority in the options available for someone buying a home. There were the 'Ameri-dream' and 'Ameri-gold' down payment assistance programs. These vanished by the end of 2007 in the panic of the sub-prime loan crash.

Then in 2009 and 2010 there were the 'First time home buyer tax credits' which the government offered for a limited time, essentially giving new home buyers a tax refund for buying a home. So government programs come and go, and so buyers can never rely too long on the existence of such programs. This fact as well makes Land Contracts a viable option for investors.

Today seller financing is still a protected right. However, if you consider many other areas of our society that have rights stripped away in recent years, anything can be thrown on the table it seems. So as an investor, consider real estate investment as a better option than the traditional stock markets, and bond markets. If you understand Land Contracts, you can be successful with it as can represent a good investment return.

There are always risks. You could lose a lot of money. However, you can lose that in the stock market and bond market as well, as many have learned in recent years. At least with real estate, you still own something tangible, and you can minimize risk by becoming well educated on the subject, making sensible well thought out purchases, and insuring everything you buy against damages. *"Always keep the door open for learning, and share what you learn from others, and in the end you will come out okay"* is something my mother always told me, and as I have gotten older, it turns out she was right.

The most important thing I tell investors that are hesitant to consider residential real estate as a place for their investment dollars, is this: *People need to live in houses.* They will either rent them, or buy them. By doing so, working people will spend often up to 50 to 60% of their earned income each month on a place to live. Why not be in a position to benefit from that with your investment dollars?

Glossary

Common Real Estate Terms

ABSORPTION RATE: Describes the ratio of the number of properties in an area that have been sold against the number available. Usually in report form to show the volatility of a market.

ABSTRACT OF TITLE: A compilation of the recorded documents relating to a parcel of land, from which an attorney may give an opinion as to the condition of the title. This system is still in use in some parts of Wisconsin and in some other states; but more often giving way to the use of the system of title insurance. (See also: *TITLE INSURANCE*)

ACCELERATION CLAUSE: A provision in a mortgage that gives the lender the right to demand *immediate payment* of the outstanding loan balance under certain circumstances. This is usually when the borrower defaults on the loan, but is can also be for other terms defined in the mortgage.

ACCREDITED BUYER REPRESENTATIVE (ABR):
A professional designation earned by REALTORS® who take advanced training in Buyer Representation offered by the Real Estate Buyer's Agent Council (REBAC). (See also: *REAL ESTATE BUYERS AGENT COUNCIL*)

ACRE: A measurement of an area of land that totals 43,560 square feet.

ACTUAL AGE: The amount of time that has passed since a building or other structure was built. (See also: *EFFECTIVE AGE*)

AD VALOREM TAX: Taxes assessed by a State, County or Municipality based on the value of the land and improvements.

ADDENDUM: A supplement to any document that contains additional information pertinent to the subject. Appraisers use an addendum to further explain items for which there was inadequate space on the standard appraisal form. Something added; a list or other material added to a document, letter, contractual agreement, escrow instructions, etc. (See also: *AMENDMENT*).

ADJUSTABLE-RATE MORTGAGE (ARM): A type of mortgage where the interest rate varies based on a particular index, normally the prime lending rate. A loan in which the rate of interest is tied to a specific financial index, with both the rate of interest and the monthly payments subject to change at established adjustment intervals of time.

ADJUSTED SALES PRICE: An opinion of a property's sales price, after adjustments have been made to account for differences between it and another comparable property.

ADJUSTED INTERVAL: This defines the period of time between the changes in the interest rate and/or monthly payment as part of an 'adjustable rate' loan. These intervals will vary depending on the lending institution and the type of loan for which application is being made.

AFFORDABILITY ANALYSIS: A calculation used to determine an individual's likelihood of being able to meet the obligations of a mortgage for a particular property. This analysis takes into account the down payment, closing costs and on-going mortgage payments, as well as the individual's financial application.

AGENCY: Any relationship in which one party (agent) acts for or represents another (principal) under the authority of the latter. Agency involving real property should be in writing, such as listings, Buyer brokerage agreements, trusts, powers of attorney, etc.

AGENT: A person who has been appointed to act on behalf of another for a particular transaction.

ALTA (American Land Title Association): An organization composed of title insurance companies which have adopted certain insurance policy forms to standardize coverage on a national basis.

AMENDMENT: A change to alter a part of an agreement without changing the principal idea or essence.

AMENITY: Any feature of a property that increases its value or desirability. These might include natural amenities such as location or proximity to mountains, or man-made amenities like swimming pools, parks or other recreation.

AMORTIZATION: The repayment of a loan through regular periodic payments. A payment breakdown for a debt, broken into installment payments; consisting of both principal and interest over a defined period of time. The origin of the word 'Amortize' derives from the Latin meaning of 'To put to death'. So Amortization ultimately means to extinguish or 'put to death' a debt or loan.

AMORTIZATION SCHEDULE: The breakdown of individual payments throughout the life of an amortized loan, showing both principal contribution and debt service (interest) fees. (See *AMORTIZATION*)

AMORTIZATION TERM: The length of time over which an amortized loan is repaid. Mortgages are commonly amortized over 15 or 30 years. (See *AMORTIZATION*)

ANNUAL PERCENTAGE RATE (APR): The rate of annual interest charged on a loan.

APPLICATION: A form used to apply for a mortgage loan that details a potential borrower's income, debt, savings and other information used to determine credit worthiness. It often requires disclosure of financial information and credit history.

APPLICATION FEE: A fee, often non-refundable, charged by the lender to cover costs of processing an application.

APPRAISAL: A "defensible" and carefully documented opinion of value usually by an appraiser. Most commonly derived using recent sales of comparable properties by a licensed, professional appraiser. A written formal estimation of the 'estimated current value' of a home.

APPRAISAL REPORT: The end result of the appraisal process, usually consists of one major, standardized form such as the Uniform Residential Appraisal Report form 1004, as well as all supporting documentation and additional detail information. The purpose of the report is to convey the opinion of value of the subject property and support that opinion with corroborating information.

APPRAISED VALUE: An opinion of the fair market value of a property (as determined by a licensed certified appraiser), following accepted appraisal principals.

APPRAISER: An educated, certified professional with extensive knowledge of real estate markets, values and practices. The appraiser is often the only independent voice in any real estate transaction with no vested interest in the ultimate value or sales price of the property.

APPRECIATION: The natural rise or increase in property value due to market forces.

APR (Annual Percentage Rate): The cost of credit expressed as a yearly rate. It takes into account interest, points and loan origination fee. Since all lenders are required to use the same guidelines in determining APR, this is a good basis for comparing the cost of various loan programs.

ARMS LENGTH TRANSACTION: Any transaction in which the two parties are unconnected and have no overt common interests. Such a transaction most often reflects the true market value of a property.

ASSESSED VALUE: This is a value assigned to real estate, for taxable purposes, by a local jurisdictional tax assessor.

ASSESSMENT: The function of assigning a value to a property for the purpose of levying taxes.

ASSESSMENT RATIO: The comparative relationship of a property's assessed value to market value.

ASSESSMENTS: (1) The estimating of value of property for tax purposes. (2) A levy against property in addition to general taxes. It can be for improvements such as streets, sewers, etc. (3) Charges against unit owners in a condominium by a condo or homeowners association.

ASSESSOR: The jurisdictional official who performs the assessment and assigns the value of a property.

ASSET: Any item of value which a person owns that is considered appreciating in value.

AUTOMATED UNDERWRITING SYSTEM (AUS): This is a computer program that allows a loan officer to enter a potential borrower's information into it from a submitted application and then reviews it. It provides an instant response as to whether the person will qualify for a loan and for which programs. It is considered to be a rapid and impartial system for preliminarily evaluating an applicant's qualification for a loan.

BALLOON MORTGAGE (OR BALLOON NOTE): A mortgage loan in which the monthly payments are not large enough to repay the loan by the end of the term. So at the end of the term, the remaining balance comes due in a single large payment.

BALLOON PAYMENT: This is the final large payment at the end of a mortgage term.

BANKRUPTCY: When a person or business is unable to pay their debts and seeks protection of the state against creditors. Bankruptcies remain on credit records for up to ten years and can prevent a person from being able to get a loan.

BENEFICIARY: A person or entity named to receive the income or property held in a trust. (See TRUST)

BILL OF SALE: A receipt indicating the sale of property. This is a written document that serves as a record, as when one transfers ownership of personal property.

BORROWER: Anyone who borrows money from a lending source.

BREACH (also called Default): Failure to comply with the terms of a contract.

BROKER (REAL ESTATE): An individual who facilitates the purchase of property by bringing together a buyer and a seller. One who engages in any of several sorts of business activities relating to the financing, rental or sale of real property or a business.

BUNGALOW: A one-story, home-style dating from the early twentieth century. This is often characterized by a low-pitched roof.

BUYER'S AGENT (REPRESENTATIVE): A Real Estate Agent that has a contractual relationship to represent a buyer in a real estate transaction.

CAPE COD COLONIAL: A single-story house style made popular in New England. This is often characterized by a steep roof with gables.

CAVEAT EMPTOR: Literally translated from Latin: *"Let the buyer beware."* A common business tenet, where it describes the buyer's responsibility for verifying any and all claims, made by the seller of the property. The buyer assumes all risk in their purchase.

CERTIFICATE OF ELIGIBILITY: A document issued by the Veterans Administration that certifies eligibility for a VA loan.

CERTIFICATE OF TITLE: A document designating the legal owner of a parcel of real estate. This is usually provided by a title or abstract of title company. (See also: *TITLE* and *ABSTRACT OF TITLE*)

CERTIFIED RESIDENTIAL SPECIALIST (CRS): A professional designation program offered to REALTORS® that requires over 70 hours of advanced training, and the sale of 25 homes to achieve. The CRS designation is offered only by the Council of Residential Specialists. (See also: *COUNCIL OF RESIDENTIAL SPECIALISTS*)

CHAIN OF TITLE: The complete history of ownership of a piece of property.

CHARGE-OFFS: Any time a creditor has closed an account and marked the account off as a loss. A designation on a credit report that an account went delinquent, and the closed the account and took it as a loss as opposed to sending it to collections.

CLEAR TITLE: Ownership of property that is not encumbered by any counter-claim or lien.

CLOSING: The process whereby the sale of a property is consummated with the buyer completing all applicable documentation, including signing the mortgage obligation and paying all appropriate costs associated with the sale (See *CLOSING COSTS*). In real estate sales, the procedure in which documents are executed and delivered in return for the payment of the sales price, and the sale (or loan) is completed.

CLOSING COSTS: Describes all appropriate costs generated by the sale of property, which the parties must pay, to complete the transaction. Costs may include appraisal fees, origination fees, title insurance, taxes and any points negotiated in the deal. One-time costs that must be paid before the loan can be "closed" or funded. These costs may include such things as property taxes, insurance, broker's fees, escrow fees, title insurance premium, deed recording fee, title insurance premium, title transfer tax, etc. Escrow instructions will stipulate which portions of the fees are to be paid by Buyer or Seller. An estimate of closing costs will be given to Buyer by the lender within a few days after receiving the loan application. (All or a portion of the closing costs may be financed depending on the loan program.)

CLOSING STATEMENT: The document detailing the final financial arrangement, complete with settlement figures, between a buyer and seller and the costs paid by each.

CO-BORROWER: A second person sharing obligation on the loan and title on the property.

COLLATERAL: An asset which is placed at risk to secure the repayment of a loan.

COLLECTION: The process a lender takes to pursue a borrower who is delinquent on his payments in order to bring the mortgage current again. This includes documentation that may be used in the foreclosure process.

COMMISSION: Compensation earned by a Real Estate Agent for negotiating a purchase or sale of property or otherwise complying with his agency contract.

COMMON AREA ASSESSMENTS: Fees which are charged to the tenets or owners of properties to cover the costs of maintaining areas shared with other tenets or owners. Commonly found in condominium, PUD or office spaces.

COMMON AREAS: Any areas, such as entryways, foyers, pools, recreational facilities or the like, which are shared by the tenets or owners of property nearby. Commonly found in condominium or office spaces.

COMPARABLES: An abbreviated term used by appraisers to describe properties which are similar in size, condition, location and amenities to a subject property whose value is being determined. The Uniform Standards of Professional Appraisal Practice (USPAP) establish clear guidelines for determining a comparable property.

COMPOUND INTEREST: Interest paid on the principal amount, as well as any accumulated interest.

CONCESSIONS: Additional value granted by a buyer or seller to entice another party to complete a deal.

CONDOMINIUM: A development where individual units are owned, but common areas and amenities are shared equally by all owners.

CONSTRUCTION LOAN: A loan made to a builder or home owner that finances the initial construction of a property, but is replaced by a traditional mortgage one the property is completed.

CONTINGENCY: Something that must occur before something else happens. Often used in real estate sales when a buyer must sell a current home before purchasing a new one. Or, when a buyer makes an offer that requires a complete home inspection before it becomes official.

CONTRACT: A legally binding agreement, oral or written, between two parties.

CONVENTIONAL MORTGAGE: A traditional, real estate financing mechanism that is not backed by any government or other agency (FHA, VA, etc.).

CONVERTIBLE ARM: A mortgage that begins and is adjustable, that allows the borrower to convert the loan to a fixed rate within a specific timeframe.

CONVEYANCE: Transfer of title to land. Includes most instruments by which interest in real estate is created, mortgaged or assigned.

COST OF FUNDS INDEX (COFI): An index of financial institutions costs used to set interest rates for some Adjustable Rate Mortgages.

COUNCIL OF RESIDENTIAL SPECIALISTS (CRS): A national organization based in Chicago, Illinois that provides advanced training for REALTORS®. The Council of Residential Specialists offers a special designation for REALTORS® called 'Certified Residential Specialist (CRS)' which is earned after over 70 hours of advanced training, and a minimum of 25 homes sold. CRS is affiliated and endorsed by the National Association of REALTORS®. Less than 4% of REALTORS® nationally earn the CRS designation.

COVENANT: A stipulation in any mortgage that, if not met, can be cause for the lender to foreclose.

CREDIT: A loan of money for the purchase of property, real or personal. Credit is either secured by an asset, such as a home, or unsecured.

CREDIT HISTORY: A record of debt and payments on such, past and present. Used by mortgage lenders in determining credit worthiness of individuals.

CREDITOR: A person to whom money is owed.

CREDIT REPORT: A detailed report of an individual's past credit performance, employment and the history of where they have lived. It is prepared by a credit bureau. Used by lenders to determine credit worthiness of individuals.

CREDIT REPOSITORY: Large companies that gather and store financial and credit information about individuals who apply for credit.

CUL-DE-SAC: A dead-end street with only one entrance/exit. Such a street is usually characterized by a circular turn-a-round at the end.

DEBT: An obligation to repay some amount owed. This may or may not be monetary.

DEBT EQUITY RATIO: The ratio of the amount a mortgagor still owes on a property to the amount of equity they have in the home. Equity is calculated at the fair-market value of the home, less any outstanding mortgage debt.

DEED: A document indicating the ownership of a property.

DEED OF TRUST: A document which transfers title in a property to a trustee, whose obligations and powers are stipulated. Often used in mortgage transactions. An instrument used in many states in place of a mortgage. Property is transferred to a trustee by the borrower (trustor), in favor of the lender (beneficiary), and re-conveyed upon payment in full.

DEED OF RECONVEYANCE: A document which transfers ownership of a property from a Trustee back to a borrower who has fulfilled the obligations of a mortgage.

DEFAULT: The condition in which a borrower has failed to meet the obligations of a loan or mortgage.

DELINQUENCY: The state in which a borrower has failed to meet payment obligations on time.

DEPOSIT: Cash given along with an offer to purchase property, also called earnest money. (See *EARNEST DEPOSIT*)

DEPRECIATION: The natural decline in property value due to market forces or depletion of resources.

DETACHED SINGLE-FAMILY HOME: A single building improvement intended to serve as a home for one family.

DISCOUNT POINTS: Points paid in addition to the loan origination fee to get a lower interest rate. One point is equal to one percent of the loan amount.

DUE-ON-SALE CLAUSE: A clause in a mortgage giving the lender the right to demand payment of the full balance when the borrower sells the property.

DUPLEX: A single-building improvement which is divided and provides two units which serve as homes to two families.

DWELLING: A house or other building which serves as a home.

DOWN PAYMENT: An amount paid in cash for a property, with the intent to mortgage the remaining amount due.

EARNEST MONEY DEPOSIT: A cash deposit made to a home seller to secure an offer to buy the property. This amount is often forfeited if the buyer decides to withdraw his offer. It shows good faith that the transaction proposal will be honored.

EASEMENT: The right of a non-owner of property to exert control over a portion or all of a property. For example, power companies often own an easement over residential properties for access to their power lines, or two properties adjacent to each other might share a common driveway.

ECONOMIC DEPRECIATION: The decline in property value caused by external forces, such as neighborhood blight or adverse development.

EFFECTIVE AGE: The subjective, estimated age of a property based on its condition, rather than the actual time since it was built. Excessive wear and tear can cause a property's effective age to be greater than its actual age.

EMINENT DOMAIN: The legal process whereby a government can take ownership of a piece of property in order to convert it to public use. Often, the property owner is paid fair-market value for the property.

ENCROACHMENT: A building or other improvement on one property which invades another property or restricts its usage.

ENCUMBRANCE: A claim against a property. Examples are mortgages, liens and easements. A claim, lien, charge, or liability attached to and binding real property. Any 'right to' or 'interest in', land which may exist in one other than the owner, but which will not prevent the transfer of fee title.

EQUAL CREDIT OPPORTUNITY ACT (ECOA): U.S. federal law requiring that lenders afford people equal chance of getting credit without discrimination based on race, religion, age, sex etc.

EQUITY: The difference between the fair market value of a property and that amount an owner owes on any mortgages or loans secured by the property.

EQUITY BUILD-UP: The natural increase in the amount of equity an owner has in a property, accumulated through market appreciation and debt repayment.

ESCROW: An amount retained by a third party in a trust to meet a future obligation. Often used in the payment of annual taxes or insurance for real property.

ESCROW ACCOUNT: An account setup by a mortgage servicing company to hold funds with which to pay expenses such as: homeowners insurance and property taxes.

ESCROW AGENT: A neutral third party, appointed to act as custodian for documents and funds.

ESCROW ANALYSIS: An analysis performed by the lender (usually once each year), to see that the amount of money going into the escrow account each month is correct for the forecasted expenses.

ESCROW DISBURSEMENTS: The payout of funds from an escrow account to pay property expenses: such as taxes and insurance.

ESTATE: The total of all property and assets owned by an individual.

ESTOPPELS: The prevention of one from asserting a legal right because of prior actions inconsistent with its assertion.

EXAMINATION OF TITLE: The report on the title of a property from the public records or an abstract of the title. (See also: *TITLE COMPANY* and *ABSTRACT OF TITLE*)

EXCLUSIVE LISTING: An agreement between the owner of a property and a real estate agent giving the agent exclusive right to sell the property.

EXECUTOR: The person named in a will to administer the estate.

FAÇADE: The front exposure of any building. This is often used to describe an artificial or false front which is not consistent with the construction of the rest of the building.

FAIR CREDIT REPORTING ACT: Federal laws, regulating the way credit agencies disclose consumer credit reports. It defines the remedies available to consumers for disputing and correcting mistakes on their credit history.

FAIR HOUSING: This refers to Federal and State laws that embrace the ideal of equal housing opportunities for everyone. *Fair Housing laws* prohibits anyone in the profession of real estate, or mortgage lending from refusing to negotiate for or engage in a real estate transaction with a person because of race, color, religion, national origin, age, sex, familial status, marital status, or mental and physical handicap. In some states, this list is further expanded to include height, weight, sexual orientation and HIV Positive. Discrimination in the terms of a rental, lease, or purchase is against the law. It also includes in the furnishing of facilities in connection with such as a transaction, such as appraising a home, property inspections, land surveys, etc. This also extends to publishing or advertising, directly or indirectly, or intent to make a limitation, specification or discrimination based on any of the categories listed above. The origin of these civil rights goes back to the Civil Rights Act of 1866. It was later expanded with the Civil Rights Act of 1968, and the later the 'Persons with Disabilities Civil Rights Act' of 1976. Many states have followed with their own civil rights acts pertaining to each state constitution.

FAIR MARKET VALUE: The price at which two unrelated parties, under no duress, are willing to transact business. Amount of money for which property will sell following negotiations between the owner of such property who will sell but is not required to sell and a proposed Buyer for such property who is not obligated to buy such property.

FANNIE MAE: A private, shareholder-owned company that works to make sure mortgage money is available for people to purchase homes. Created by Congress in 1938, Fannie Mae is the nation's largest source of financing for home mortgages.

FEDERAL DEPOSIT INSURANCE CORPORATION (FDIC): The U.S. Government agency created in 1933 which maintains the stability of and public confidence in the nation's financial system by insuring deposits and promoting safe and sound banking practices.

FEDERAL HOUSING ADMINISTRATION (FHA): A sub-agency of the U.S. Department of Housing and Urban Development created in the 1930's to facilitate the purchase of homes by low-income, first-time home buyers. It currently provides federally-subsidized mortgage insurance for private lenders.

FHA MORTGAGE: A mortgage that is insured by the Federal Housing Administration (FHA).

FICO: 'FICO' is an acronym for 'Fair, Isaac and Company'. Fair, Isaac & Co. developed the credit scoring system that is used today by the three major credit bureaus: Experian, TransUnion and Equifax.

FIRST MORTGAGE: The description of the primary loan or mortgage secured by a piece of property.

FIXED-RATE MORTGAGE (FRM): A mortgage which has a fixed rate of interest over the life of the loan.

FIXTURE: Any piece of personal property which becomes permanently affixed to a piece of real property. It generally refers to property that it attached to the home, such as light fixtures, toilets, counter tops, etc.

FLOOD INSURANCE: This describes supplemental insurance which covers a home owner for any loss due to water damage from a flood. This is often required by lenders for homes located in federally designated flood zones.

FLOODPLAIN: The extent of the land adjoining water which, because of its topography, would flood if the water overflowed its banks.

FLOOR PLAN: The representation of a building which shows the basic outline of the structure, as well as detailed information about the positioning of rooms, hallways, doors, stairs and other features. Often includes detailed information about other fixtures and amenities.

FORECLOSURE: The process whereby a lender can claim the property used by a borrower to secure a mortgage and sell the property to meet the obligations of the loan.

FORFEITURE: The loss of property or money due to the failure to meet the obligations of a mortgage or loan secured by that property.

FUNCTIONAL OBSOLESCENCE: A decrease in the value of property due to a feature or lack thereof which renders the property undesirable. Functional obsolescence can also occur when the surrounding area changes, rendering the property unusable for it's originally intended purpose.

GENERAL LIEN: A broad-based claim against several properties owned by a defaulting party.

GOVERNMENT MORTGAGE: Any mortgage insured by a government agency, such as the FHA or VA.

GRANTEE: Any person who is given ownership of a piece of property by another party or entity.

GRANTOR: Any person who gives away ownership of a piece of property.

HAZARD INSURANCE: This is insurance covering damage to a property caused by hazards such as fire, wind and accident.

HAZARDOUS MATERIALS: Substances that may be hazardous to health (i.e., asbestos, radon gas, lead based paint).

HOME EQUITY LINE OF CREDIT (HELOC): A type of mortgage loan that allows the borrower to draw cash against the equity in his home.

HOME INSPECTION: A complete examination of a building to determine its structural integrity and uncover any defects in materials or workmanship which may adversely affect the property or decrease its value.

HOME INSPECTOR: A person who performs professional home inspections. This is usually a professional with an extensive knowledge of houses and their construction methods. Their knowledge will also include common house problems, how to identify those problems and how to correct them.

HOMEOWNER'S ASSOCIATION: An organization of home owners in a particular neighborhood or development formed to facilitate the maintenance of common areas and to enforce any building restrictions or covenants.

HOMEOWNER'S INSURANCE: A policy which covers a home owner for any loss of property due to accident, intrusion or hazard.

HOMEOWNER'S WARRANTY: An insurance policy covering the repair of systems and appliances within the home for the coverage period.

HUD-1 SETTLEMENT STATEMENT: A standardized, itemized list, published by the U.S. Department of Housing and Urban Development (HUD), of all anticipated CLOSING COSTS connected with a particular property purchase.

IMPROVEMENTS: Any item added to vacant land with the intent of increasing its value or usability.

INCOME PROPERTY: A piece of property whose highest and best use is the generation of income through rents or other sources.

INDEMNIFY: To make payment for a loss.

INDEPENDENT APPRAISAL: An estimation of value created by a professional, certified appraiser with no vested interest in the value of the property.

INDEX: Used by lenders to calculate the interest adjustments on adjustable rate loans. Some indexes are more volatile than others; this can affect adjustments in the interest rate and, subsequently, the monthly payment. Because these indexes reflect the general movement of interest rates, they tend to keep the rate on an adjustable rate loan in line with market conditions.

INITIAL RATE: An interest rate charged for the first six or twelve months of an adjustable rate loan. Normally this rate will be lower than prevailing fixed market rates.

INSPECTION: The examination of a piece of property, its buildings or other amenities.

INSTALLMENT LOAN: A line of credit for a fixed sum, with pre-set monthly payments including principle and interest. Example: loans for vehicles or equipment.

INSURABLE TITLE: The title to property which has been sufficiently reviewed by a title insurance company, such that they are willing to insure it as free and clear.

INTEREST RATE: A percentage of a loan or mortgage value that is paid to the lender as compensation for loaning funds.

INTEREST RATE CAP: A safeguard built into an adjustable rate loan to protect the consumer against dramatic increases in the rate of interest and, consequently, in the monthly payment. For example, an adjustable rate loan may have a two percentage point limit per year on the amount of increase or decrease, as well as a five percentage point limit (increase or decrease) over the life of the loan.

INTERIM FINANCING: Temporary financing usually for construction or bridge loans to facilitate the purchase of a new home before the sale of the previous home has been closed.

INVESTMENT PROPERTY: Any piece of property that is expected to generate a financial return. This may come as the result of periodic rents or through appreciation of the property value over time.

JOINT TENANCY: A situation where two or more parties own a piece of property together. Each of the owners has an equal share, and may not dispose of or alter that share without the consent of the other owners.

JUDGMENT: An official court decision. If the judgment requires payment from one party to another, the court may put a lien against the payees property as collateral.

JUDICIAL FORECLOSURE: A type of foreclosure conducted as a civil suit in a court of law.

JUNIOR MORTGAGE: A mortgage, such as a second mortgage, which is subordinate as security to another mortgage.

LAND CONTRACT: Describes an installment contract for the sale of land. The Seller (vendor) has legal title until paid in full. The Buyer (vendee) has equitable title during the contract term. See the Author's other book: *Understanding Land Contract Homes: In Pursuit of the American Dream.*

LATE CHARGE: An extra charge, or penalty added to a regular mortgage payment when the payment is made late by an amount of time specified in the original loan document.

LATENT DEFECTS: Any defect in a piece of property which is not readily apparent, but which has an impact of the value. Structural damage or termite infestation would be examples of latent defects.

LEASE: A contract between a property owner and a tenant specifying the payment amount, terms and conditions, as well as the length of time the contract will be in force.

LEASE OPTION: A lease agreement that gives the tenant an option to buy the property. Usually, a portion of the regular monthly rent payment will be applied towards the down payment.

LEGAL DESCRIPTION: The description of a piece of property, identifying its specific location in terms established by the municipality or other jurisdiction in which the property resides. This is often related in specific distances from a known landmark or intersection.

LEGAL NOTICE: The notice required by law in a particular case. It may be actual notice, constructive notice, etc.

LENDER: In real estate, the person or entity who loans funds to a buyer. In return, the lender will receive periodic payments, including principal and interest amounts. It can also be any person or organization that loans money to a borrower.

LENGTH OF CREDIT HISTORY: The length of time a borrower has had established credit accounts that are reported on his/her credit report.

LIABILITIES: A person's outstanding debt obligations.

LIABILITY INSURANCE: Insurance that covers against potential lawsuit brought against a property owner for alleged negligence resulting in damage to another party.

LIEN: Any claim against a piece of property resulting from a debt or other obligation.

LISTING AGENT: The term for a Real Estate agent that has an 'exclusive right to sell' contract with a seller to sell their home. The home is considered to be 'listed' for sale through a Real Estate agent.

LOAN: Money borrowed, to be repaid with interest, according to the specific terms and conditions of the loan.

LOAN OFFICER: A person that "sells" loans, representing the lender to the borrower, and the borrower to the lender.

LOAN ORIGINATION: How a lender refers to the process of writing new loans.

LOAN SERVICING: The processing of payments, mailing of monthly statements, management and disbursement of escrow funds, etc. Typically carried out by the loan company you make payments to.

LOAN-TO-VALUE RATIO (LTV): The comparison of the amount owed on a mortgaged property to its fair market value.

LOCK-IN: An agreement between a lender and a borrower, guaranteeing an interest rate for a loan if the loan is closed within a certain amount of time.

LOCK-IN PERIOD: The amount of time the lender has guaranteed an interest rate to a borrower.

MANUFACTURED HOUSING: Once known as "mobile homes," manufactured housing is any building which has been constructed off site, then moved onto a piece of real property.

MATURITY: The date on which the principal balance of a financial instrument becomes due and payable.

MERGED CREDIT REPORT: A credit report derived from data obtained from multiple credit agencies. This usually is contains information from all three credit bureaus in a single report.

METES AND BOUNDS: A traditional way of describing property, generally expressed in terms of distance from a known landmark or intersection, and then following the boundaries of the property back to its origin.

MILL RATE: A percentage applied to the assessed valuation to determine taxes.

MORTGAGE: A financial arrangement wherein an individual borrows money to purchase real property and secures the loan with the property as collateral.

MORTGAGE BANKER: This describes a financial institution that provides primary and secondary mortgages to home buyers.

MORTGAGE BROKER: This is a person or organization that serves as a middleman to facilitate the mortgage process. Brokers often represent multiple mortgage bankers and offer the most appropriate deal to each buyer.

MORTGAGEE: The entity that lends money in a real estate transaction.

MORTGAGE INSURANCE: This describes a policy that fulfills the obligations of a mortgage when the policy holder defaults, or is no longer able to make payments. The policy protects the mortgage lender.

MORTGAGE INSURANCE PREMIUM (MIP): A fee that is often included in mortgage payments that pays for mortgage insurance coverage.

MORTGAGE LIFE INSURANCE: A policy that fulfills the obligations of a mortgage when the policy holder dies.

MORTGAGE NOTE: A promissory note secured by a mortgage and executed by mortgagor at the same time as the mortgage for the amount stated in the mortgage, with the legal description of land described in the mortgage also stated in such note.

MORTGAGOR: The entity that borrows money in a real estate transaction.

NEIGHBORHOOD: 1) A community, district or area especially with regards to some point of reference. 2) The people living near and around a community.

NOTE: A legal document that obligates a borrower to repay a mortgage loan at a stated interest rate during a specified period of time.

NOTICE OF DEFAULT: Formal written notice from a lender to a borrower that default has occurred.

OCCUPANCY: A physical presence within and control of a property.

OLD TERMITE ACTIVITY: Where no termites are currently active, but indications of past activity can be seen.

OPEN ACCOUNTS: Credit accounts that are open and still in use by a borrower. Accounts considered active and in use by the creditor.

OWNER OCCUPIED: The state of property wherein the owner occupies at least some portion of the property.

PAYMENT HISTORY: The running record of a borrowers' performance on paying back borrowed funds.

PERSONAL PROPERTY: Owned items which are not permanently affixed to the land.

PERSONAL OR 'PRINCIPLE' RESIDENCE: The primary domicile where a person or family lives.

PITI: Refers to 'principal', 'interest', 'taxes', and 'insurance'. This describes the complete monthly home loan payment, inclusive of taxes and insurance.

PLAT: A plan or chart of a piece of land which lays out existing or planned streets, lots or other improvements.

POINT: A percentage of a mortgage amount (one point = 1 percent).

POINTS AND FEES: A point is a charge equal to one percent of the principal amount of the loan (e.g., 2 points charged on a $100,000 loan would> equal $2,000). Points are generally payable at closing and may be paid by the Buyer or Seller, or split between them. In addition, a flat dollar amount fee may also be charged. Under some lending programs, a buyer may be allowed to include these points and fees as part of the total amount financed.

PRE-APPROVAL: The process of applying for a mortgage loan and becoming approved for a certain amount at a certain interest rate before a property has been chosen. Pre-approval allows the borrower greater freedom in negotiations with sellers. It does not mean they have been fully approved for a loan, but just states they have met the preliminary lending requirements and been told so by a lender.

PREPAYMENT: Payment made that reduces the principal balance of a loan before the due date and before the loan has become fully amortized.

PREPAYMENT CLAUSE: Clause in mortgage, mortgage note or land contract providing that debtor may pay more than agreed installment payment at any time.

PREPAYMENT PENALTY: A fee that may be charged to a borrower who pays off a loan before it is due.

PRE-QUALIFICATION: Less formal that pre-approval, pre-qualification usually means a written statement from a loan officer indicating his or her opinion that the borrower will be able to become approved for a mortgage loan.

PRIME RATE: The interest rate that a bank and other lending institutions charge other banks or preferred customers.

PRINCIPAL: The amount owed on a mortgage which does not include interest or other fees.

PRINCIPAL BALANCE: The outstanding balance of principal on a mortgage. This does not include the amount of total interest due.

PRIVATE MORTGAGE INSURANCE (PMI): A form of mortgage insurance provided by private, non-government entities. This is normally required when the loan to value ratio is less that 20%. The premium is paid by the borrower and is included in the mortgage payment. (See also: *LOAN TO VALUE RATIO*)

PROCESSING (TURNAROUND) TIME: The amount of time required from the day loan application documents are submitted in full to the day the loan closes and loan funds are disbursed. This is the total processing time for a home loan.

PROPERTY: Any item which is owned or possessed.

PRO-RATE: To allocate between Seller and Buyer their proportionate share of an obligation paid or due.

PUBLIC RECORDS: Any record recorded by a County or State. These can include judicial records, bankruptcies, foreclosures, deeds, etc.

PURCHASE AGREEMENT: A written contract signed by the buyer and seller stating the terms and conditions under which a property will be sold.

QUIT-CLAIM DEED: A legal document which transfers any ownership an individual has in a piece of property. Often used when the amount of ownership is not known or is unclear.

RANCH HOUSE: An architectural style typified by a single-story, low-roof construction popular in the western U.S.

RATE LOCK (OR GUARANTEE): A guarantee from a lender of a specific interest rate for a period of time.

REAL ESTATE: A piece of land and any improvements or fixtures located on that land.

REAL ESTATE AGENT: A licensed professional who facilitates the buying and selling of real estate.

REAL ESTATE BUYERS AGENT COUNCIL (REBAC): A national organization that offers a special designation for REALTORS® on Buyer Representation in real estate transactions. To earn the designation requires approximately 40 hours of training, in addition to participating in at least 5 transactions as a Buyers Representative. The designation offered by REBAC is entitled 'Accredited Buyer Representative (ABR)' (See also: *ACCREDITED BUYER REPRESENTATIVE*)

REAL ESTATE SETTLEMENT PROCEDURES ACT (RESPA): A federal law requiring lenders to give full disclosure of closing costs to borrowers.

REAL PROPERTY: Land, improvements and appurtenances, and the interest and benefits thereof.

REALTOR®: A designation given to a real estate licensee who is a member of a board associated with the National Association of REALTORS®.

RECORDER: A local government employee whose role it is to keep records of all real estate transactions within the jurisdiction.

RECORDING: The filing of a real estate transaction with the appropriate government agent. A real estate transaction is considered final when it is recorded. (See *RECORDER*)

REMAINING BALANCE: The amount of principal, interest and other costs that has not yet been repaid.

RESIDENTIAL PROPERTY: A piece of property whose highest and best use is the maintenance of a residence.

REVOLVING CREDIT: A type of credit that allows the borrower to make charges against a predetermined line of credit. The customer then pays monthly installments on the amount borrowed, plus interest. Example: Credit Cards are considered revolving lines of credit.

RURAL: An area outside of an established urban area or metropolitan district.

SALE PRICE: The actual price a property sells for, exclusive of any special financing concessions.

SECOND MORTGAGE: A loan secured by the equity in a home, when a primary mortgage already exists.

SECURED LOAN: This is a loan that is backed by collateral. In the case of a mortgage loan, the collateral is the house.

SEPTIC INSPECTION: An inspection of the septic system of a given property. Sometimes this is a required inspection for closing in a contract.

SERVICING: Mortgage bankers typically retain the right to collect monthly payments and take care of any customer problems. They send a payment to the investor each month. For this service, the mortgage banker receives a small fee (1/4% to 1/2% of the mortgage amount).

SINGLE-FAMILY PROPERTY: A property designed and built to support the habitation of one family.

SUBDIVISION: A residential development that is created from a piece of land which has been subdivided into individual lots.

SUBJECT PROPERTY: This is a term which indicates a property which is being appraised.

SURVEY: A specific map of a piece of property which includes the legal boundaries and any improvements or features of the land. Surveys also depict any rights-of-way, encroachments or easements.

SWEAT EQUITY: The method whereby a home owner develops equity in a property, either during the purchase or throughout its life, by personally constructing improvements rather than paying to have them built.

TERM: The number of years before a loan is scheduled to be paid off. 15-year and 30-year terms are most common.

TERMITE LETTER: An official letter from a certified pest inspection company. The letter states that a property has been inspected and found to have been treated, or free and clear of termite infestation. Some States require such a letter for all real estate closings before transfer of title can occur.

TITLE: A specific document which serves as proof of ownership.

TITLE COMPANY: An organization which researches and certifies ownership of real estate before it is bought or sold. Title companies also act at the facilitator ensures all parties are paid during the real estate transaction.

TITLE INSURANCE: A policy which insures a property owner should a prior claim arise against the property after the purchase has been completed. This also covers a lender should a question of ownership arise.

TITLE SEARCH: The process whereby the Title Company researches a properties title history and ensures that no outstanding claims exist.

TRANSFER OF OWNERSHIP: Any means by which the ownership of a property changes hands.

TRANSFER OF TAX: Taxes payable when title passes from one owner to another.

TRANSFER TAX OR TRANSFER FEE: A tax on the transfer of real property. Generally based on value of property being transferred (i.e., purchase price). Check statutes for each state. This is also called 'Documentary Transfer Tax' in some States.

TRUST: A legal entity created by a 'Trustor' to place an estate or property in the care of another called a 'Trustee'. A Trustee oversees the responsibility to manage a Trust for the benefit of the 'Beneficiary', who is the party that will receive the estate or property if the Trust is dissolved.

TRUSTEE: A fiduciary who holds or controls property for the benefit of another.

TRUSTOR: A person who creates a Trust. (See *TRUST*)

TRUTH IN LENDING: A federal law requiring full disclosure by lenders to borrowers of all terms, conditions and costs of a mortgage.

TUDOR: A style of architecture typified by exposed stone, wood and brick construction. This is similar in style to English manor homes.

UNDERLYING FINANCING: A mortgage, deed of trust, land contract etc. Prior to (underlying) a land contract, mortgage, etc. on the same property.

UNDERWRITER: This is a person who works for a lending or some other financial company, and oversees the process of a loan, and makes sure a borrower who is applying complies and conforms to the guidelines as defined by the institution they work for. They often have final approval or disapproval authority on any application.

UNENCUMBERED PROPERTY: Any property which has no outstanding claims or liens against it.

USURY: Charging more than the legal rate of interest for the use of money.

VA GUARANTEE MORTGAGE: A mortgage that is guaranteed by the Department of Veterans Affairs (VA).

VETERANS AFFAIRS, DEPARTMENT OF (VA): The successor to the Veteran's Administration, this government agency is responsible for ensuring the rights and welfare of our nation's veterans and their dependents. Among other duties, the VA insures home loans made to veterans.

VESTING: Name(s) in which title property is held.

WALK-THROUGH INSPECTION: A process whereby an appraiser examines a property in preparation for estimating its value. Also, the process of inspecting a property for any damage prior to that property being bought or sold. Sometimes called a 'final walk-through' when buyers do a final review or tour of a home prior to closing.

WARRANTY: An affidavit given to stipulate the condition of a property. The person giving the warranty assumes liability if the condition turns out to be untrue.

WARRANTY DEED: This is a deed used in many states to convey fee title to real property. Until the widespread use of title insurance, the warranties by the grantor were very important to the grantee. When title insurance is purchased, the warranties become less important as a practical means of recovery by the grantee for defective title.

WEAR AND TEAR: A term used to indicate the normal damage inflicted on a property through every-day use.

WELL INSPECTION: An official inspection of the water quality and functionality of a well system. This is sometimes a required inspection for a closing in some States.

ZONE: A specific area within a municipality or other jurisdiction which conforms to certain guidelines regarding the use of property in the zone. Typical zones include single-family, multi-family, industrial, commercial and mixed-use.

Useful Links & References

❧

Foreclosure Laws by State:

www.realtytrac.com/foreclosure-laws/foreclosure-laws-comparison

Online Legal Websites for Real Estate forms:

Legal Zoom

www.legalzoom.com

Rocket Lawyer

www.rocketlawyer.com

Law Depot

www.lawdepot.com

Nolo

www.nolo.com

U.S. Legal Forms

www.USLegalForms.com

Legalwiz

www.legalwiz.zom

Resources for Selling a Land Contract:

Amerifunds

www.amerifunds.us

Mortgage Note Buyer US

www.mortgagenotebuyer.us

Cash Flow Connection Pro LLC

www.cashflowconnectionpro.net

Credit Report:

Annual Credit Report

www.annualcreditreport.com

My Fico

www.MyFICO.com

Credit Repair Information:

Federal Trade Commission Consumer Information on Credit Repair: www.consumer.ftc.gov

Reports on Credit Repair: www.BankRate.com

1031 Tax Deferred Exchanges:

1031 Tax Deferred Exchange Made Simple

www.1031exchangemadesimple.com

1031.org FAQ Page

www.1031.0rg/about1031/faq.htm

1031 Investing inside a Roth IRA

www.1031fec.com/RithIRA.htm

1031 Exchange Advantage FAQ Page

www.1031exchangeadvantage.com

1031 Exchange Institute

www.1031exchangeinstitute.org

Acknowledgments

❧❧

I have come to realize there are so many people behind every project I take on in life, and seldom do they get acknowledged for all their behind the scenes support in projects like these. With this second published work, I have many people to thank.

In my research into publishing eBooks, I came across a man named **Nitin Mistry** who developed software to make it easy and simple to self publish an eBook. His software is called: *The Ultimate e-Book Creator* and you can look it up online by clicking on the name here: **www.ultimateebookcreator.com.**

I would like to personally thank and acknowledge him in this second book, for without his help I would not have been able to publish my first book. As of this writing, we have never spoken personally, but have corresponded through email throughout the process on several occasions.

The *National Association of Realtors* has also been a magnificent organization to be a part of, and the I have learned so much from my colleagues in this business over the years that I once again would like to acknowledge all of them. Realtors are across the country and around the globe open the door of homeownership to millions every day, and are the greatest professionals. I am so proud and humbled to be a member of this magnificent group.

On a personal note, I would like to thank my friend **Sue Fairchild,** who has always been supportive of me when I mentioned this project to her.

As well, special acknowledgment and thank you is due my step-daughter **Juana Salamanca** for her support, friendship and words of encouragement whenever I have mentioned my writing projects.

Special thanks also goes to my sister **Jeanne Matheny** who has been openly supportive to me over the years whenever I mentioned or discussed with her my ambitions of becoming writer. Also I would like to thank my brother **Richard Delaware,** a professor at the University of Kansas City MO who was one of my very first customers who purchased my first eBook to support my writing career.

Finally, my wife **Margarita Delaware** has been my lifeline whenever I ran into difficulty, or strayed too far off course in more than just my ambitions as a writer. She is the love of my life, and my greatest supporter.

About the Author

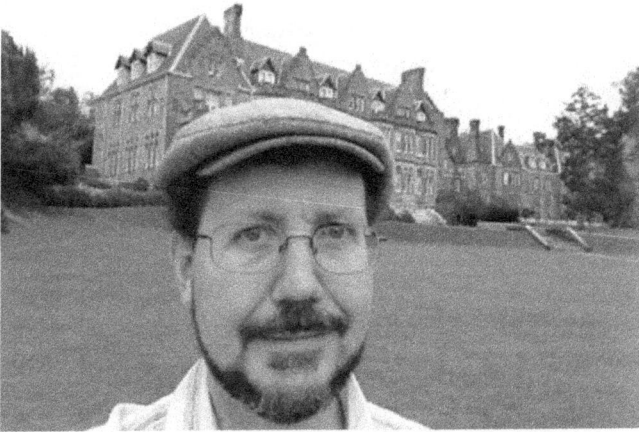

Michael Delaware is a Phoenix, Arizona native who now resides in Battle Creek, Michigan with his wife Margarita. He also lived in Georgia for 15 years in the 1980's and 1990's where he owned and operated a stained and beveled glass studio in the Metro-Atlanta area. During those years he was an active volunteer in the community, coordinating annual Arts and Crafts Festivals in the downtown district of Roswell, Georgia. He also participated in Arts & Crafts Shows for over 25 years as a vendor in numerous States. He has been a Michigan resident since 1999.

His other published works include numerous non-fiction books on real estate, sales management, marketing and other self-help topics. He has also published fiction and non-fiction stories for children

As an illustrator and photographer, he has included his works in his own books and blogs. He enjoys hiking and mountain biking in the great outdoors and taking long walks in the woods with his dog.

Currently he is an active Realtor in Michigan and frequent community volunteer. He is a member of the National Association of Realtors, The Council of Residential Specialists, and the Michigan Association of Realtors. He is also an active member of the Battle Creek Area Association of Realtors where he was awarded 'Realtor of the Year' in 2010, and served as Board President in 2011. He founded his own independent publishing company in 2012.

To follow Michael:

www.MichaelDelaware.com

Facebook.com/MichaelDelawareAuthor

Amazon.com/Author/MichaelDelaware

Linkedin.com/in/MichaelDelaware

@MichaelDelaware

Other titles by the author available as eBooks:

The Art of Sales Management: Lessons Learned on the Fly *(also available in paperback)*

The Art of Sales Management: Revelations of a Goal Maker *(also available in paperback)*

The Art of Sales Management: 75 Training Drills to Build Confidence, Excellence & Teamwork *(also available in paperback)*

Small Business Marketing: An Insider's Collection of Secrets *(also available in paperback)*

Arts & Craft Shows: The Top 10 Mistakes Artist Vendors Make... And How to Avoid Them! *(also available in paperback)*

Arts & Craft Shows: 12 Secrets Every Artist Vendor Should Know *(also available in paperback)*

Inspiration: The Journey of a Lifetime

For Real Estate:

Understanding Land Contract Homes: In Pursuit of the American Dream

Going Home... Renting to Home Ownership in 10 Easy Steps

In Children's Fiction:

Scary Elephant Meets the Closet Monster

In Children's Non-Fiction:

My Name is Blue: The Story of a Rescue Dog

More titles will be available in print in late 2013 and in 2014. For a current list of available print books visit:

www.ifandorbutpublishing.com

If you found this book on real estate useful, you might also like these other titles by the same author:

www.IfAndorButPublishing.com